Introduction

" The Importance of a Business Mindset in Everyday Life"

In a world driven by innovation, competition, and constant change, having a business mindset isn't just a tool for entrepreneurs or CEOs—it's an essential approach that can help anyone thrive in various aspects of life. Whether you're leading a team, navigating personal finances, or simply trying to make better decisions, thinking like a businessperson equips you with a mindset that fosters growth, problem-solving, and strategic thinking.

A business mindset transcends beyond the boardroom and applies to everyday life, enabling you to see opportunities where others may see obstacles, make informed decisions, and create value in the spaces you occupy. It's about understanding how to analyze risks, manage resources, and stay adaptable in an ever-changing environment. Essentially, it helps you develop a framework that empowers you to be proactive, rather than reactive, no matter the context.

This chapter will explore why cultivating a business mindset can give you an edge in not just achieving financial success, but also in enhancing personal development and relationships. By embracing this mindset, you'll begin to view the world differently—not just as a collection of daily tasks or challenges, but as an interconnected ecosystem where strategy, vision, and execution play pivotal roles.

Throughout this book, you'll discover how to unlock your potential by integrating key business principles into your everyday decisions and actions. We'll begin by uncovering why a business-oriented approach is crucial for anyone who aspires to live a successful, impactful life.

Overview

In this chapter, we delve into the significance of adopting a business mindset in all facets of daily life. Often, people associate business thinking solely with entrepreneurship or corporate leadership, but its principles are universally applicable. A business mindset is about strategic thinking, adaptability, resource management, and problem-solving—skills that can enrich both personal and professional aspects of life.

The chapter highlights how individuals can benefit from approaching everyday decisions with the same mindset used by successful businesspeople. Whether it's managing personal finances, navigating career choices, or fostering relationships, adopting a business-oriented perspective allows for better planning, improved risk management, and more effective decision-making.

Key concepts such as viewing challenges as opportunities, maximizing value, and remaining proactive rather than reactive are introduced. The chapter sets the foundation for understanding how incorporating business principles into your thinking can lead to long-term success, both in work and in personal growth. It emphasizes that a business mindset isn't just for those in the corporate world, but for anyone seeking to excel and make informed, impactful decisions in life.

Chapter 1: Understanding the Business Mindset

To build a successful business or think like a businessman, it's essential to understand the mindset that drives entrepreneurship. This chapter delves into the core of what a business mindset is and how cultivating it can set you on the path to success.

What is a Business Mindset?

A business mindset is a way of thinking that consistently seeks opportunities, takes calculated risks, and focuses on creating value. It is not simply about making money but about developing strategies, solving problems, and creating something meaningful for the long term. The mindset drives people to be visionaries, innovators, and leaders in their industries.

Businessmen often have certain qualities that allow them to turn ideas into realities. They see opportunities where others see obstacles, think in terms of growth, and always have an eye on their goals. Understanding this mindset requires breaking down its key components:

1. Vision

2. Risk Tolerance

3. Resilience

4. Problem-Solving

5. Adaptability

6. Focus on Value Creation

7. Growth-Oriented Thinking

1. Vision: The Core of a Business Mindset

At the heart of every successful businessman is a strong vision. A vision is not just a goal or a plan; it's a long-term picture of where you want to go and how you see your business evolving over time. It's the roadmap that helps you navigate the ups and downs of entrepreneurship.

Businessmen don't just think about immediate returns. They plan for the future. Whether you're thinking of starting a business or scaling one, having a clear vision helps you stay focused on the end goal. But vision alone isn't enough—you need the discipline to break that vision into actionable steps and constantly remind yourself why you started in the first place.

To develop a business mindset, you need to:

- Set a clear, long-term vision that aligns with your passions and values.

- Regularly reassess and adjust your vision to adapt to changing market conditions or personal growth.

- Stay motivated by visualizing the impact of your vision on your customers, employees, and society.

2. Risk Tolerance: The Willingness to Take Calculated Risks

A major aspect of the business mindset is being comfortable with uncertainty. Every business venture involves risk—whether financial, emotional, or reputational. However, successful businessmen don't shy away from risks; they embrace them, but in a calculated way. Risk-tolerance isn't about gambling your resources on a whim but making informed decisions that have the potential for high rewards.

Understanding risk in business is about:

- Knowing the difference between calculated risks and reckless risks: Entrepreneurs evaluate the potential downsides and decide if the risk is worth the reward.

- Managing risk: This could mean starting small and scaling, diversifying income streams, or having contingency plans in place.

- Learning from failure: Not all risks will pay off, but businessmen use failures as opportunities to learn and grow.

3. Resilience: Bouncing Back from Setbacks

The entrepreneurial journey is full of challenges. Rejection, failure, and uncertainty are all part of the game. What sets successful businessmen apart is their resilience—the ability to bounce back from setbacks and keep moving forward. They don't see failure as the end but as a necessary step toward success.

Building resilience means developing the mental strength to face difficulties without giving up. Businessmen know that setbacks are temporary and that perseverance is the key to overcoming obstacles. They develop a thick skin and learn to navigate both internal and external pressures.

To build resilience, entrepreneurs often:

- Cultivate a strong support system, whether it's mentors, friends, or peers in their industry.

- Focus on continuous learning and personal development, seeking ways to improve both personally and professionally.

- Keep a positive outlook, even in the face of adversity. They maintain a growth mindset, understanding that failure is not a reflection of their ability but a part of the learning process.

4. Problem-Solving: Seeing Problems as Opportunities

At its core, business is about solving problems. The best businesses are those that find a gap in the market and provide solutions. Entrepreneurs with a business mindset thrive in problem-solving environments. They don't shy away from challenges; instead, they see them as opportunities to innovate and improve.

For instance, when customers express dissatisfaction, a businessman doesn't view it as criticism but as feedback for how the product or service can be better. The more problems they solve, the more value they create for their business.

To develop strong problem-solving skills, businessmen:

- Ask the right questions: They dig deep to understand the root causes of issues, whether in their business operations, market trends, or customer behavior.

- Stay curious: The best entrepreneurs are constantly learning, whether it's new technologies, business models, or industry insights.

- Think creatively: They look for unconventional solutions, often stepping outside of the traditional playbook to solve problems in new ways.

5. Adaptability: Thriving in a Changing Environment

The business landscape is constantly evolving. Whether it's due to technological advancements, changing consumer preferences, or economic shifts, businessmen need to be adaptable to survive and thrive.

Having an adaptable mindset means being open to change, learning new skills, and adjusting strategies as needed. Entrepreneurs who are too rigid often get left behind, while those who embrace flexibility and innovation are better positioned for long-term success.

To foster adaptability, businessmen often:

- Embrace change: They don't fear new trends or shifts in the market. Instead, they seek to understand them and determine how to leverage them for their advantage.

- Diversify their skills: Entrepreneurs who succeed long-term invest in themselves. Whether it's learning new software, understanding financial models, or developing leadership skills, they never stop growing.

- Stay agile: Businessmen regularly evaluate their business models and strategies to ensure they are keeping up with market trends and consumer needs.

6. Focus on Value Creation: Beyond Profit

While profit is certainly a key driver for any business, it's not the only goal of a true businessman. A business mindset goes beyond the bottom line and focuses on creating value for customers, employees, and the wider community.

Successful entrepreneurs understand that businesses exist to serve their customers. They focus on meeting the needs of their audience in a way that is both meaningful and sustainable. This approach not only drives profitability but also builds brand loyalty, trust, and long-term success.

To focus on value creation, businessmen:

- Prioritize customer needs: Every decision is made with the customer in mind. They continually seek ways to improve their product or service to better solve customer problems.

- Invest in their team: A great businessman knows that a strong team is vital to success. They invest in their employees' growth, create a positive work environment, and build a culture of collaboration and innovation.

-Think long-term: Value-driven businesses don't just aim for short-term profits but for long-term impact. Entrepreneurs with this mindset are willing to invest in their business's future, even if it means delaying immediate gains.

7. Growth-Oriented Thinking: Constant Improvement and Innovation

A businessman is always focused on growth—both personal and professional. They constantly seek ways to expand their business, whether through new product lines, entering new markets, or improving internal processes. Growth-oriented thinking is about pushing beyond the status quo and never becoming complacent.

Entrepreneurs with a growth mindset are always looking for opportunities for innovation. They stay ahead of the curve by anticipating changes in the market, leveraging new technologies, and staying in tune with consumer demands.

To develop a growth-oriented mindset, businessmen:

- Set ambitious goals: They challenge themselves and their team to continuously improve and aim for bigger targets.

- Foster a culture of innovation: Businessmen encourage creativity within their organizations, welcoming new ideas and approaches to solving problems.

- Keep learning: Growth-oriented entrepreneurs are lifelong learners. They read, attend conferences, network, and seek out mentors who can help them expand their knowledge and perspectives.

Practical Steps to Cultivating a Business Mindset;

Now that you understand the core elements of a business mindset, it's time to put them into action. Here are some practical steps you can take to develop this way of thinking:

1. Start with self-awareness: Understand your strengths, weaknesses, passions, and motivations. Know what drives you and where you want to go.

2. Set clear, long-term goals: Break these down into actionable, short-term steps to keep you focused and motivated.

3. Learn from successful businessmen: Read biographies, attend seminars, and follow the leaders in your industry to understand their thought processes and strategies.

4. Take calculated risks: Step outside your comfort zone, but always evaluate the potential outcomes before taking action.

5. Develop resilience: Embrace failure as a learning opportunity. Reflect on setbacks and use them as a stepping stone to future success.

6. Keep improving your problem-solving skills: Practice thinking critically about challenges you face in your business or personal life. Over time, you'll become more adept at finding solutions.

7. Stay adaptable: Be open to learning and change. Regularly reassess your strategies and be willing to pivot when necessary.

8. Focus on adding value: Whether through your product, service, or relationships, always seek to provide value to those around you.

9. Cultivate a growth mindset: Never stop learning. Stay curious and embrace new opportunities for personal and professional growth.

Definition and Characteristics of a Business Mindset

In today's fast-paced and highly competitive world, developing a business mindset is crucial for anyone seeking success—whether you're an entrepreneur, a leader, or a professional working within a company. A business mindset doesn't just come naturally; it must be cultivated. This mindset defines how you think, approach problems, and make decisions that align with your long-term goals.

In this chapter, we will explore what it means to have a business mindset, break down its definition, and examine the key characteristics that are common in individuals who possess it. By the end of this chapter, you'll not only understand what constitutes a business mindset, but also learn the core attributes that help successful business people excel.

1. What is a Business Mindset?

A business mindset is a specific way of thinking that drives individuals to make decisions that maximize business opportunities, solve problems strategically, and take calculated risks. It is not limited to owning or running a business—it is a set of perspectives and habits that can be applied to any role within an organization.

At its core, a business mindset focuses on creating value, driving growth, and leveraging resources effectively. It includes the ability to balance short-term results with long-term goals, maintaining an entrepreneurial spirit while being grounded in data-driven decisions. Essentially, it is a mindset where the individual constantly seeks opportunities, remains adaptable, and understands the importance of efficiency, productivity, and customer satisfaction.

To put it simply, a business mindset is:

- **Opportunity-focused**: Always on the lookout for growth or improvement.
- **Problem-solving oriented**: Capable of diagnosing issues and creating solutions.
- **Strategic**: Balancing risks and rewards with long-term goals in mind.
- **Value-driven**: Focused on maximizing value for the company, customer, and stakeholders.

2. Key Characteristics of a Business Mindset

Now that we have a general understanding of what a business mindset is, let's dive deeper into the traits and characteristics that embody this way of thinking. Cultivating these characteristics will equip you to approach business challenges more effectively and unlock greater potential for success.

A. Growth-Oriented Thinking

The most fundamental characteristic of a business mindset is a growth-oriented perspective. This means having the belief that abilities, intelligence, and skills can be developed through effort, learning, and persistence. People with a fixed mindset believe that talent or intelligence alone determines success, while those with a business mindset understand that continuous improvement and adaptation are essential.

- **Continuous learning**: A business-minded individual never stops learning. Whether through formal education, hands-on experience, or mentorship, they seek knowledge constantly.
- **Adaptability**: Markets, industries, and technologies change. A person with a business mindset is not resistant to change but instead embraces it, adjusting their strategies as needed to stay ahead.

B. Goal-Oriented

One of the primary distinctions of a business mindset is the focus on clear, measurable goals. Successful business leaders always work toward defined objectives, both in the short and long term. These goals guide their decisions and actions.

- **Vision and Purpose**: Individuals with a business mindset often have a clear vision of where they want to go. They set long-term goals and ensure that their short-term efforts align with these objectives.
- **Execution-focused**: It's not enough to set goals; you need to be able to execute them. Having a business mindset means being driven to turn ideas into reality through strategic planning and consistent effort.

C. Problem-Solving Ability

Business is about solving problems. The better you are at identifying and resolving issues, the more successful you will be. A business mindset encourages people to approach challenges as opportunities for growth and innovation.

- **Proactive approach**: Rather than waiting for problems to arise, individuals with a business mindset anticipate them and create preemptive solutions.
- **Creative thinking**: Solving problems requires creativity and thinking outside the box. Often, the most effective solutions are those that go beyond conventional wisdom.

D. Risk Tolerance and Resilience

Running or growing a business often involves taking calculated risks. People with a business mindset are not afraid of taking risks, but they do so with careful thought and preparation. Risk is seen as an opportunity for reward, rather than something to be avoided.

- **Calculated risks**: A person with a business mindset does not take risks blindly. They assess the potential rewards and the worst-case scenarios before making decisions.
- **Resilience**: Business is full of challenges, and setbacks are inevitable. The ability to bounce back from failure and learn from mistakes is a hallmark of a strong business mindset.

E. Resourcefulness

Resourcefulness is key to a business mindset. It involves making the most of what you have, whether that's capital, talent, or time. Successful business people can turn limited resources into significant opportunities by finding creative solutions.

- **Maximizing efficiency**: Whether it's managing finances or human resources, a business mindset emphasizes maximizing efficiency. Every decision is evaluated in terms of return on investment.
- **Leverage**: People with a business mindset know how to leverage partnerships, technology, and other resources to their advantage, helping them get more done with less.

F. Customer-Centric Approach

A successful business mindset always puts the customer at the center. Whether you're selling products, services, or ideas, understanding and addressing the needs of your audience is paramount.

- **Empathy**: Business success is built on relationships. A business mindset fosters a deep understanding of customer pain points and desires.
- **Value creation**: Instead of merely selling a product or service, a person with a business mindset seeks to create value for customers. This leads to long-term loyalty and business growth.

G. Data-Driven Decision Making

A business mindset relies heavily on data and analytics to inform decisions. This is essential for reducing risks, optimizing operations, and identifying growth opportunities.

- **Analyzing trends**: People with a business mindset pay attention to market trends, consumer behaviors, and financial reports to guide their strategies.
- **Informed choices**: While intuition plays a role, major business decisions are often backed by data, ensuring more reliable outcomes.

H. Networking and Relationship Building

A business mindset includes a keen focus on networking and relationship building. Successful business people understand the value of building and maintaining strong connections within their industry and community.

- **Collaboration**: A business mindset is inherently collaborative. Working well with others—both inside and outside your organization—is key to unlocking opportunities.
- **Partnerships**: Whether it's forming strategic alliances, finding mentors, or fostering partnerships, business-minded individuals understand the power of relationships in growing their business.

I. Strategic Thinking

Long-term success in business requires more than just quick fixes or reacting to the situation at hand. A business mindset involves thinking strategically—considering long-term objectives, potential risks, and the wider landscape in which the business operates.

- **Big-picture focus**: A person with a business mindset can zoom out and understand how various elements—market trends, competition, internal dynamics—come together to influence their business.
- **Adaptability**: Strategic thinking also means being flexible. When market conditions shift, someone with a business mindset knows how to pivot and alter their strategies accordingly.

J. Accountability

Finally, a key aspect of a business mindset is accountability. Individuals with this mindset take ownership of their decisions, both good and bad. They don't shift blame;

instead, they accept responsibility for their actions and learn from them.

- **Self-discipline**: A business-minded person is disciplined and holds themselves to a high standard. They are focused on their goals and make daily efforts to achieve them.
- **Ownership mentality**: Whether they are the boss or an employee, individuals with a business mindset approach their role as if they own the company. This sense of responsibility drives them to give their best.

3. Why Developing a Business Mindset Matters

Developing a business mindset isn't just about thriving in a professional setting—it's about excelling in life. This mindset allows you to tackle challenges more effectively, stay motivated, and continuously seek improvement. It helps you navigate uncertainty, take ownership of your actions, and stay focused on creating value, which ultimately leads to both personal and professional growth.

In a world where change is the only constant, having a business mindset is your anchor. It gives you the confidence to innovate, push boundaries, and pursue your goals with conviction, no matter what obstacles lie in your path.

Thinking How the Business Mindset Differs from Traditional

In today's rapidly evolving world, the way successful businesspeople think and operate has shifted dramatically from the traditional mindset that most people are taught. While conventional education often emphasizes security, stability, and gradual progress, the business mindset revolves around adaptability, innovation, and risk-taking. This chapter will delve into the core differences between traditional thinking and the business mindset, highlighting how adopting this entrepreneurial perspective can lead to unparalleled opportunities for growth, success, and fulfillment.

1. Risk Versus Security

One of the most defining differences between traditional and business thinking is the attitude toward risk. Traditional thinking emphasizes minimizing risks in life, often focusing on securing a stable job, saving money cautiously, and avoiding situations that could lead to financial loss or instability. This stems from a mindset of scarcity, where the goal is to preserve what one has worked for.

In contrast, the business mindset embraces calculated risks as a necessary part of growth. Entrepreneurs and business leaders understand that to achieve extraordinary results, one must step out of the comfort zone. Instead of fearing failure, they view it as an opportunity to learn and grow. In fact, many of the world's most successful businesspeople credit their failures as stepping stones to their ultimate success. They embrace uncertainty and understand that with high risk comes high reward.

> **Example**: A person with traditional thinking might save money in a secure savings account, whereas a business-minded individual might invest that money into a startup or a new venture with the potential for much greater returns.

2. Scarcity Versus Abundance

Traditional thinking often operates on the principle of scarcity. This mindset suggests that resources are limited and that to succeed, one must conserve and protect what they have.

People raised with this mindset may see success as a zero-sum game, where someone else's gain is their loss.

The business mindset, however, is rooted in abundance. Entrepreneurs believe that opportunities are endless and that wealth, success, and resources can always be created. They understand that markets can expand, new products can be invented, and collaboration often leads to mutual growth. This abundance mindset encourages innovation, creativity, and collaboration, as opposed to the competition-focused, protectionist approach of traditional thinking.

> **Example**: In a traditional mindset, employees may compete for promotions, seeing their colleagues as rivals. In a business mindset, entrepreneurs seek partnerships and joint ventures, understanding that collaboration can create more wealth and opportunities for everyone involved.

3. Linear Growth Versus Exponential Growth

Traditional thinking is linear in nature. In schools and workplaces, progress is often measured in a step-by-step process — studying hard, getting good grades, securing a job, and slowly climbing the corporate ladder. This thinking is deeply ingrained in most people and promotes the belief that success is achieved gradually, one small step at a time.

The business mindset, on the other hand, focuses on exponential growth. Entrepreneurs are always looking for ways to scale rapidly, often through leveraging technology, building systems, or employing others. Instead of climbing a slow and steady path, they look for ways to achieve massive growth quickly by disrupting industries or identifying market inefficiencies.

> **Example**: Traditional employees may work overtime to increase their salary incrementally, whereas entrepreneurs build systems that allow them to earn income even while they sleep, such as through passive investments or scalable businesses.

4. Focus on Problems Versus Focus on Solutions

Traditional thinking often focuses heavily on problems. People with this mindset tend to dwell on obstacles and limitations, seeing them as barriers to success. This can lead to a mindset of defeat or resignation, where individuals are more likely to believe that external factors control their lives.

In contrast, the business mindset is solutions-oriented. Entrepreneurs train themselves to look at problems as opportunities for innovation. Instead of being bogged down by challenges, they ask, "How can I solve this?" This proactive approach often leads to the creation of new products, services, or processes that address the problem at hand. In business, every problem represents a market need waiting to be filled.

> **Example**: During the COVID-19 pandemic, traditional businesses struggled with the sudden shift to remote work, while business-minded entrepreneurs quickly launched virtual meeting platforms, home delivery services, and remote work tools to meet the growing demand.

5. Job Security Versus Value Creation

Traditional thinking often prioritizes job security and stability. Many people are raised with the belief that finding a secure job with good benefits is the ultimate goal. This mindset values long-term employment, loyalty to a single employer, and a predictable paycheck.

On the other hand, the business mindset prioritizes value creation over job security. Entrepreneurs know that their worth in the marketplace is directly tied to the value they create for others. Instead of relying on an employer for security, they create their own by identifying gaps in the market and delivering solutions that customers need. This mindset encourages individuals to take control of their destiny by becoming creators and innovators rather than relying on a corporation for stability.

Example: A traditionally-minded individual might strive for a promotion in a company to ensure long-term job security, while a business-minded person might build a product or service that solves a real-world problem, thereby creating wealth and security through entrepreneurship.

6. Time as a Cost Versus Time as an Asset

In traditional thinking, time is often viewed as a cost. People trade their time for money in a job, believing that working harder or longer hours will ultimately lead to success. This approach reinforces the idea that time is finite, and once it's spent, it's gone.

The business mindset, however, treats time as an asset — one that can be leveraged. Entrepreneurs understand that they cannot scale their efforts by solely trading time for money. Instead, they build systems, hire employees, and invest in automation to free up their time while generating income. By leveraging time, businesspeople can focus on high-impact tasks that lead to growth and success, rather than spending time on repetitive, low-value activities.

Example: A traditional thinker might work longer hours to earn a larger paycheck, while an entrepreneur might delegate tasks or automate processes to focus on strategic decisions that increase the company's profitability.

7. Education as a Destination Versus Lifelong Learning

Traditional thinking often regards education as a destination. People are encouraged to get formal education, earn degrees, and then rely on those qualifications for the rest of their careers. Once formal education is complete, many people stop actively seeking to learn or grow their skill sets, believing that they have "finished" their education.

In contrast, the business mindset embraces lifelong learning. Entrepreneurs understand that the world is constantly changing and that they must continuously adapt to new trends, technologies, and market demands. They seek out mentors, read books, attend seminars, and engage in self-education to stay ahead of the curve. Learning is not seen as something to be completed but as an ongoing process essential to personal and professional growth.

> **Example**: A traditional thinker may stop learning after completing a college degree, whereas an entrepreneur continually invests in personal development through courses, workshops, and real-world experience to keep up with changing market dynamics.

Chapter 2: Goal Setting for Success

Setting goals is the foundation for achieving success, whether in personal development, career growth, business ventures, or any other aspect of life. Without clear, actionable goals, even the most talented individuals can find themselves drifting, lacking direction, or falling short of their true potential. In this chapter, we will explore the art of goal setting for success, outlining practical strategies, proven techniques, and the mindset required to turn your dreams into reality.

Goal setting is more than just deciding what you want to achieve. It's a strategic process that involves understanding your desires, planning the steps to attain them, overcoming obstacles, and staying committed even when the journey becomes challenging. As we dive into this chapter, we'll explore why goal setting is crucial, how to set effective goals, and ways to maintain focus and motivation.

1. Why Goal Setting Matters

The importance of goal setting cannot be overstated. Goals serve as a roadmap to guide you toward your vision of success. They provide a sense of purpose, motivation, and direction, ensuring that you're consistently moving forward rather than getting stuck in unproductive routines.

Here's why goal setting is critical for success:

a. Clarity and Focus

When you set a clear goal, you give your brain a target to aim for. It's like inputting a destination into a GPS. Without a clear goal, your actions and decisions may become scattered and inconsistent, making it difficult to know where to invest your time and energy.

b. Motivation

Goals fuel motivation. They provide something tangible to strive for, pushing you to take action, even when the path seems challenging. The satisfaction of moving closer to your goal creates a positive feedback loop, encouraging you to keep going.

c. Accountability

Setting goals holds you accountable. Whether you're accountable to yourself, a mentor, or a team, having a set target gives you a reason to measure your progress and make adjustments when necessary.

d. Self-Improvement

Goal setting fosters continuous self-improvement. As you work toward your goals, you develop new skills, habits, and mindsets that prepare you for future challenges. Every goal you set and achieve builds momentum, boosting your confidence and capabilities.

2. Types of Goals

Before diving into the process of setting goals, it's essential to understand that there are different types of goals, each with its own function and significance. Knowing which type of goal to focus on at different stages can help you plan more effectively.

a. Short-Term Goals

Short-term goals are the immediate steps you take to progress toward your larger objectives. These goals are typically achievable within a few days, weeks, or months and serve as building blocks toward more significant achievements. They help break down long-term aspirations into manageable, actionable tasks.

> **Example**: If you want to start a business, a short-term goal could be to conduct market research or create a business plan within the next 30 days.

b. Long-Term Goals

Long-term goals require more time and effort to achieve, often spanning several years. These are your big-picture aspirations that align with your vision for the future. Long-term goals guide your decision-making and overall strategy, giving you something to strive for in the long run.

> **Example**: If you want to become a successful entrepreneur, a long-term goal could be to build a thriving company within the next five years.

c. Outcome Goals

Outcome goals focus on the result or the desired end-state you want to achieve. While they provide direction, outcome goals can be challenging to control because they often depend on external factors.

> **Example**: An outcome goal could be to increase your company's revenue by 50% in the next year. However, factors like market conditions, competition, and consumer demand can influence this goal.

d. Process Goals

Process goals emphasize the actions and behaviors needed to achieve a desired outcome. These goals are entirely within your control, making them more manageable and realistic. They also help you focus on the journey, rather than just the destination.

> **Example**: If your outcome goal is to increase revenue, a process goal might be to implement a new marketing strategy or improve customer service.

e. Performance Goals

Performance goals are measurable and specific benchmarks that gauge your progress toward an outcome. These are often related to specific tasks, skills, or results that you can directly influence.

> **Example**: A performance goal could be to make five sales calls per day or to complete a certification course within six months.

3. The SMART Framework for Goal Setting

One of the most effective ways to set clear, actionable goals is by using the SMART framework. This method ensures that your goals are well-defined and realistic, increasing the likelihood of success.

a. Specific

Your goal should be clear and specific. Vague goals can lead to confusion, making it difficult to track your progress. A specific goal outlines exactly what you want to accomplish and leaves no room for ambiguity.

> **Example**: Instead of setting a goal like "I want to improve my marketing skills," a specific goal would be "I will enroll in a digital marketing course and complete it within three months."

b. Measurable

A measurable goal includes criteria that allow you to track your progress. This helps you stay motivated and understand when you're moving closer to achieving your goal.

> **Example**: If your goal is to increase your business's social media presence, a measurable goal might be "I will increase the number of followers on Instagram by 20% over the next two months."

c. Achievable

Your goal should be realistic and attainable. While it's essential to challenge yourself, setting goals that are impossible or too difficult can lead to frustration and burnout.

> **Example**: If you're just starting a business, it might not be realistic to aim for $1 million in revenue in your first year. Instead, an achievable goal could be to acquire your first 100 customers within six months.

d. Relevant

Your goal should align with your broader objectives and aspirations. Ensure that it is relevant to your overall mission and contributes to your long-term vision.

> **Example**: If your long-term goal is to become a thought leader in your industry, a relevant short-term goal could be to start writing guest articles for industry blogs or speaking at local events.

e. Time-Bound

A time-bound goal includes a deadline or a specific time frame for completion. Without a deadline, it's easy to procrastinate or lose focus.

> **Example**: Instead of setting a vague goal like "I want to grow my business," a time-bound goal would be "I will open three new stores within the next two years."

4. The Role of Vision and Purpose in Goal Setting

While SMART goals are essential for structuring your objectives, they need to be driven by a clear vision and sense of purpose. Vision is the long-term, aspirational picture of where you want to be, and purpose is the reason why you want to achieve it.

a. Crafting a Vision

Your vision should be bold, inspiring, and future-oriented. It reflects the highest potential version of yourself and your business. A well-crafted vision statement can guide your goal-setting process and keep you motivated during challenging times.

> **Example**: A personal vision might be "To become a leader in sustainable business practices and inspire a new generation of eco-conscious entrepreneurs."

b. Understanding Your Purpose

Purpose gives meaning to your goals. It answers the question, "Why do I want to achieve this?" Without purpose, even well-structured goals can feel empty, leading to burnout or lack of fulfillment.

> **Example**: If your goal is to expand your business, your purpose might be to create more jobs in your community, support local suppliers, or provide innovative solutions to customers.

5. Breaking Down Goals Into Actionable Steps

Once you've set your SMART goals, the next step is to break them down into smaller, actionable tasks. Large goals can be overwhelming, and without a clear plan, you may struggle to make consistent progress.

a. Create Milestones

Milestones are smaller checkpoints that help you track your progress toward your main goal. They break down large goals into manageable tasks, providing a clear sense of direction and achievement.

> **Example**: If your goal is to write a book, a milestone might be to complete the first draft within three months, followed by editing and publishing.

b. Develop a Timeline

A timeline creates structure and accountability, ensuring that you're staying on track. Set deadlines for each milestone, and regularly review your progress.

> **Example**: If you want to launch a new product in one year, you might set specific deadlines for product development, market testing, and promotional campaigns.

c. Prioritize Tasks

Not all tasks are equally important. Use prioritization techniques like the Eisenhower Matrix or the Pareto Principle (80/20 rule) to focus on high-impact tasks that move you closer to your goal.

> **Example**: If your goal is to increase your online presence, prioritize tasks like optimizing your website and creating valuable content over less impactful tasks like tweaking your logo design.

6. Overcoming Obstacles and Staying Committed

Achieving goals requires resilience, as you will inevitably encounter obstacles along the way. Successful individuals stay committed to their goals even when faced with setbacks.

a. Anticipate Challenges

Before you embark on your goal-setting journey, take the time to anticipate potential obstacles. This proactive approach helps you develop strategies to overcome them.

> **Example**: If you know that time management is a challenge, plan to delegate non-essential tasks or use productivity tools to stay organized.

b. Develop a Growth Mindset

A growth mindset is essential for overcoming setbacks. Instead of viewing failure as a reflection of your abilities, see

The Significance of Setting Clear, Measurable Goals

Setting clear, measurable goals is one of the most powerful tools for achieving success in any area of life. Whether you're pursuing personal growth, striving for career advancement, or building a business, clearly defined goals help direct your energy, focus, and resources toward your desired outcome. Without goals, it's easy to get distracted, lose motivation, or feel overwhelmed by the enormity of the tasks ahead. This chapter explores why setting clear, measurable goals is so important and how it can transform your journey toward success.

1. Goals Provide Clarity and Direction

The first and most crucial benefit of setting clear goals is the clarity they provide. Clarity is the foundation of effective action, as it ensures you know exactly what you are aiming for. Vague or undefined goals leave room for uncertainty, which can lead to confusion and indecision.

When you set a clear goal, you define exactly what success looks like. You move from thinking in generalities—like wanting to "be successful" or "make more money"—to thinking in specifics. For example, rather than saying, "I want to grow my business," a clear goal would be, "I want to increase my revenue by 25% over the next 12 months by launching a new product line."

Having a well-defined goal sharpens your focus and eliminates unnecessary distractions. Every decision, action, and resource can now be aligned with your specific objective. Instead of wasting time on unimportant tasks, you prioritize activities that directly contribute to achieving your goal.

> **Example**: If your goal is to save $10,000 for a down payment on a house in one year, you now have a clear financial target that allows you to make better decisions about your spending, savings, and budgeting.

2. Measurable Goals Track Progress

Measurable goals are essential for tracking progress. If a goal isn't measurable, you can't objectively determine whether you're moving closer to achieving it or not. Having measurable goals allows you to track and evaluate your progress regularly, which keeps you motivated and informed about where you stand.

Measurable goals provide tangible markers that help break large objectives into smaller, manageable steps. This not only makes the journey less overwhelming but also creates a sense of achievement as you check off each milestone along the way. By seeing measurable progress, you stay engaged and motivated to keep pushing forward.

> **Example**: If your goal is to lose 20 pounds in three months, you can track progress by measuring your weight weekly. Each pound lost represents a measurable step toward your final goal, making the process more encouraging and reinforcing your commitment.

Tracking measurable goals also enables you to identify what's working and what isn't. If you aren't making the expected progress, you can adjust your approach, change tactics, or seek additional resources to get back on track.

3. Goals Enhance Focus and Productivity

When goals are clear and measurable, they enhance your focus by helping you concentrate on what truly matters. In a world full of distractions, goal setting acts as a filter for your priorities. It allows you to distinguish between tasks that are critical to your success and those that are simply time-consuming but unproductive.

Without clear goals, it's easy to fall into the trap of "busyness" rather than productivity. People often spend their days tackling an endless list of tasks without making meaningful progress toward their aspirations. Clear, measurable goals change this dynamic by giving your actions purpose and direction.

By focusing your efforts on tasks that directly contribute to your goals, you optimize your productivity. This ensures that you're not just working hard but working smart, maximizing your output and results.

> **Example**: If you are working toward completing a book, setting a measurable goal of writing 500 words per day gives you a focused, daily task that brings you closer to completing your manuscript. This structure helps you avoid distractions and prevents procrastination.

4. Goals Boost Motivation and Commitment

Motivation is critical for success, especially when challenges arise or the journey feels long. Clear, measurable goals act as powerful motivators because they give you a sense of purpose and direction. They answer the "why" behind your actions and give you something tangible to strive for.

A well-defined goal serves as a reminder of what you want to achieve and why you're willing to invest time and effort. When setbacks occur, a clear goal helps you stay committed and pushes you to persevere. Instead of feeling lost or overwhelmed, you're able to refocus on the steps needed to reach your desired outcome.

Measurable goals, in particular, fuel motivation by providing immediate feedback. Each small achievement, each incremental gain, adds to your momentum and builds confidence. The more progress you see, the more motivated you become to continue.

> **Example**: If your goal is to save money for a trip, setting a measurable goal of saving $500 per month provides clear checkpoints. Every time you hit that target, you feel a sense of accomplishment that encourages you to stay on track.

5. Goals Improve Decision-Making

Clear, measurable goals also serve as a powerful decision-making tool. When you have a specific target in mind, it becomes easier to evaluate options and make choices that align with your objectives. You are more likely to make decisions that contribute to your success rather than being swayed by short-term temptations or distractions.

> **Example**: If your goal is to launch a new business, having a measurable target like securing five clients in the first six

> months helps you decide where to allocate your time, money, and energy. Rather than getting sidetracked by tasks that don't contribute to client acquisition, you can focus on networking, marketing, and product development.

Your goals become a filter for determining whether an opportunity or action will bring you closer to or farther from your desired outcome. This leads to more intentional, strategic decision-making that accelerates your progress toward success.

6. Goals Foster Accountability

One of the key elements of setting measurable goals is that they create accountability. When you set a specific target, you make a commitment to yourself (and sometimes to others) to achieve that goal. This sense of responsibility drives you to follow through on your actions and stay disciplined, even when it's challenging.

Sharing your goals with others can increase accountability further. When you tell someone about your goal, whether it's a friend, mentor, or team member, you create a social contract. They become aware of your intentions and may check in on your progress, holding you accountable to the commitments you've made.

> **Example**: If you're working on launching a fitness program and set a measurable goal to have it ready within three months, telling a friend or business partner about your deadline creates external accountability. Knowing that others are watching your progress can increase your determination to stay on track.

Accountability is crucial for long-term success because it helps you stay consistent and overcome periods of low motivation. Whether through self-accountability or external support, having measurable goals keeps you committed to your vision.

7. Goals Encourage Continuous Improvement

Clear, measurable goals push you to improve continuously. When you set specific targets, you create a standard for yourself to strive toward. Even after achieving your initial goals, the process of setting measurable benchmarks encourages you to raise the bar and aim for higher levels of success.

By regularly reviewing and adjusting your goals, you can adapt to changing circumstances, refine your strategies, and identify areas for growth. This cycle of setting, achieving, and revising goals promotes lifelong learning and personal development.

> **Example**: After reaching a goal of increasing your company's revenue by 20%, you might set a new goal to expand into a new market or develop a new product line, ensuring that you're always growing and evolving.

8. The Power of Measurable Goals in Business

In the world of business, measurable goals are indispensable. They provide a clear framework for teams and individuals to align their efforts with the organization's overall objectives. Measurable goals help businesses track performance, identify areas for improvement, and ensure that resources are being used effectively.

Businesses that set clear, measurable goals are better equipped to navigate uncertainty and stay competitive. By setting key performance indicators (KPIs) and measurable targets, companies can assess their progress and make data-driven decisions to optimize their operations.

> **Example**: A company aiming to increase customer retention might set a measurable goal of reducing customer churn by 10% over the next year. This goal would guide the company's

strategy, encouraging improvements in customer service, product quality, or loyalty programs.

Techniques for Effective Goal Setting

Goal setting is one of the most powerful tools that successful people use to channel their energy, time, and resources. Whether you're starting a business, developing a personal brand, or planning for your future, clearly defined goals give you direction and motivation. However, many people struggle with achieving their goals because they don't set them in a way that is actionable or realistic. In this chapter, we will explore practical techniques for setting effective goals, including the SMART goals framework and the use of vision boards to visually manifest your ambitions.

Why Goal Setting Matters

Before diving into the specific techniques, let's first establish the importance of goal setting. Without a clear destination, it's easy to get lost or distracted. Goals help you prioritize what's important and provide a roadmap for how to get there. They also offer several key benefits:

1. **Clarity of Focus**: Goals give you a sense of purpose and clarity. You know exactly what you're working towards, which helps you stay focused and avoid distractions.
2. **Motivation**: When you have a goal, especially one that's meaningful to you, it becomes a powerful source of motivation. Each step you take brings you closer to achieving it, driving you to keep going even when things get tough.
3. **Measurable Progress**: A well-defined goal allows you to track your progress. This lets you see how far you've come and whether you're on the right track, allowing for adjustments along the way.

4. **Accountability**: Sharing your goals with others or writing them down helps to keep you accountable. It's a psychological commitment that increases the likelihood of follow-through.

Now that we've established the importance of goal setting, let's look at two of the most effective techniques for setting and achieving your goals: the SMART framework and vision boards.

The SMART Goals Framework

The SMART goals framework is widely recognized as one of the most effective ways to set clear, actionable goals. It turns abstract ambitions into tangible plans by breaking them down into five key components: Specific, Measurable, Achievable, Relevant, and Time-bound.

1. Specific

The first step in setting an effective goal is to make it specific. A vague goal such as "I want to grow my business" lacks clarity. What kind of growth are you looking for? Financial growth? Customer base? Operational expansion? A more specific goal might be: "I want to increase my monthly sales revenue by 20% within the next six months."

A specific goal answers the questions:

- What exactly do you want to achieve?
- Why is this goal important?
- Who is involved?
- Where will it happen?
- Which resources or constraints are involved?

2. Measurable

If you can't measure a goal, how will you know when you've achieved it? To make a goal measurable, you need to define concrete criteria for tracking progress. This usually involves numbers or metrics. For example, instead of saying, "I want to gain more clients," say, "I want to acquire five new clients within the next quarter."

Questions to ask:

- How much or how many?
- How will I know when it is accomplished?

3. Achievable

Your goal should stretch you out of your comfort zone, but it should also be realistic. Setting goals that are too far-fetched can lead to frustration and demotivation. For example, if you're just starting a new business, it might not be feasible to set a goal of making $1 million in your first year. Instead, an achievable goal might be to make $100,000 in the first year, based on market research and your business model.

Achievable goals keep you motivated because they feel within reach, but still challenging enough to push your limits.

4. Relevant

Your goals should align with your broader life or business objectives. If you set a goal that doesn't connect to your overall mission, you might waste time and resources. For example, if your goal is to become a marketing expert but you spend all your time learning unrelated skills, you may lose sight of your main objective.

Ask yourself:

- Does this goal align with my long-term plans?

- Is this the right time to pursue it?
- Does it fit with my other priorities?

5. Time-bound

Every goal needs a deadline. Without a time frame, there's no sense of urgency, and you might keep pushing the goal further into the future. A time-bound goal gives you a clear target to work toward and encourages you to prioritize. For example, instead of saying, "I want to launch my website," say, "I will launch my website by December 1st."

Time-bound goals answer the questions:

- When will I achieve this goal?
- What can I do today, this week, or this month to make progress?

By making your goals SMART, you transform them from vague ideas into well-defined objectives with a clear action plan. However, while SMART goals are essential, they focus primarily on the logical and measurable aspects of goal setting. Let's now explore a more visual and emotionally charged approach: vision boards.

Vision Boards: Manifesting Your Dreams Visually

While SMART goals help you create a detailed action plan, vision boards tap into your creativity and emotions, allowing you to see and feel your goals in a more intuitive way. A vision board is a collage of images, words, and phrases that represent your dreams and aspirations. It serves as a daily reminder of what you're working towards and helps you visualize your success.

How Vision Boards Work

The human brain responds strongly to visual stimuli. By seeing your goals represented visually, you create emotional connections to those goals, making them feel more real and attainable. Vision boards also engage your subconscious mind, helping you stay motivated and focused on your dreams.

Steps to Create a Vision Board

1. **Clarify Your Goals**: Before you start gathering materials for your vision board, you need to be clear about what you want to achieve. Use your SMART goals as a foundation. What images or words come to mind when you think about achieving these goals?
2. **Collect Materials**: Gather magazines, printed images, inspiring quotes, or any other materials that visually represent your goals. You can also use online tools or apps to create digital vision boards.
3. **Arrange Your Vision**: Organize your images and words on a board or a digital space in a way that feels meaningful to you. There's no right or wrong way to do this—just go with what feels inspiring. Some people group their images by categories, such as "career," "health," or "relationships," while others prefer a more random, creative arrangement.
4. **Display Your Board**: Once your vision board is complete, place it somewhere you will see it daily, such as your office or bedroom. The more often you see it, the more likely you are to stay focused on your goals.
5. **Review and Update**: As you achieve your goals or as your priorities change, don't hesitate to update or create a new vision board. This is an evolving tool that should reflect your current aspirations.

The Power of Visualization

Vision boards are powerful because they help you maintain a positive and forward-looking mindset. When combined with a strong action plan, they can serve as a constant reminder of your "why"—the deeper reason behind your goals. Every time you see your vision board, you reconnect with your dreams and reignite your passion for achieving them.

Combining SMART Goals and Vision Boards for Maximum Impact

While SMART goals provide the practical steps for achieving your objectives, vision boards bring those objectives to life. By combining the two, you create a balanced approach to goal setting that engages both your logical mind and your emotions.

Here's how you can use both techniques in harmony:

1. **Set SMART Goals First**: Start by defining your goals using the SMART framework. This gives you a clear, actionable roadmap.
2. **Create a Vision Board**: Once your SMART goals are in place, create a vision board that reflects the emotions and imagery associated with those goals. This helps you stay emotionally connected and inspired.
3. **Regularly Review Both**: Revisit your SMART goals periodically to track progress and make adjustments. At the same time, look at your vision board daily to keep yourself motivated and focused.

Chapter 3: Embracing Risk and Failure

Risk and failure are two inevitable aspects of life, particularly in business and personal growth. Many people fear them, often avoiding situations where the chance of failure seems high. However, successful individuals and thriving entrepreneurs understand that embracing risk and learning from failure are key components of success. In this chapter, we will explore why taking calculated risks and facing failure head-on are essential for growth, how to develop a healthy relationship with failure, and practical strategies for managing risk effectively.

Why Risk and Failure Are Necessary for Success

Before diving into strategies for embracing risk and failure, let's first understand why they are crucial for success. The fear of failure can paralyze us, but without taking risks, there is no potential for growth. Whether you're launching a new business, developing an innovative product, or taking a significant step in your personal life, risk is always present.

Here's why risk and failure are so important:

1. **Growth Happens Outside Your Comfort Zone**: Staying in your comfort zone may feel safe, but it leads to stagnation. Risk forces you to step into unknown territory, where true growth occurs. Whether it's learning new skills, developing resilience, or discovering new opportunities, growth comes from stretching yourself beyond your current limits.
2. **Failure Teaches Valuable Lessons**: Every failure carries a lesson that can help you refine your approach. When you fail, you learn what doesn't work, which helps you move closer to finding what does. Many successful entrepreneurs, including those who've built

billion-dollar empires, failed multiple times before achieving their breakthroughs.
3. **Innovation Requires Risk**: Innovation and creativity thrive in environments where risks are taken. Whether it's disrupting an industry or creating a new product, groundbreaking ideas often come from those who are willing to take risks and challenge the status quo. Risk fosters experimentation, leading to unique solutions and forward-thinking strategies.
4. **Resilience Is Built Through Failure**: Facing failure builds mental toughness. It teaches you how to persevere, recover, and try again. This resilience is critical for long-term success because every journey is full of ups and downs. The key is to learn how to bounce back and continue pushing forward.

Now that we've established the importance of risk and failure, let's explore how you can embrace them with confidence and turn them into powerful tools for success.

Changing Your Mindset: Viewing Failure as Feedback

One of the most critical shifts you can make is to change the way you view failure. Many people see failure as a sign of inadequacy, but in reality, failure is feedback. When you experience failure, it's not a reflection of your worth or abilities, but rather an indication that something didn't go as planned. Use this feedback to improve your strategy, make adjustments, and try again.

Here are some key mindset shifts to embrace failure effectively:

1. Reframe Failure as a Learning Opportunity

Instead of viewing failure as a negative outcome, see it as a step forward. Every time you fail, you gain new insights that you wouldn't have had otherwise. For example, if a business idea flops, analyze the reasons why it didn't work. Was it poor market timing? Did you target the wrong audience? Did your execution lack focus? These lessons are invaluable and will serve you in future endeavors.

2. Detach Your Self-Worth from the Outcome

It's easy to internalize failure and feel like it reflects who you are. However, it's important to separate your sense of self-worth from the outcome of your efforts. Everyone, even the most successful individuals, experiences failure at some point. Instead of letting failure define you, focus on how you respond to it. The most important thing is not whether you fail, but how you bounce back.

3. Embrace a Growth Mindset

A growth mindset is the belief that abilities and intelligence can be developed through hard work and dedication. People with a growth mindset see challenges and failures as opportunities to grow, while those with a fixed mindset view them as obstacles. By adopting a growth mindset, you become more open to taking risks because you understand that failure is part of the learning process.

4. Celebrate Your Efforts, Not Just the Results

While achieving success is the ultimate goal, it's important to recognize the value of effort. Celebrate the fact that you took action, even if the outcome wasn't what you hoped for. Acknowledging your willingness to take risks and try new things will build your confidence and motivate you to keep moving forward.

The Power of Calculated Risk-Taking

While embracing risk is essential, it doesn't mean taking reckless chances. Successful risk-taking involves careful planning, research, and strategy. This is what we call "calculated risk-taking." It's about weighing the potential benefits against the possible downsides and making informed decisions based on data, experience, and intuition.

Here's how to take calculated risks:

1. Conduct Thorough Research

Before taking any significant risk, gather as much information as possible. This might involve market research, customer feedback, financial analysis, or studying competitors. The more informed you are, the better you can assess the potential risks and rewards. For instance, if you're considering launching a new product, research the demand, costs, and potential return on investment (ROI) before diving in.

2. Assess the Worst-Case Scenario

When contemplating a risk, always consider the worst possible outcome. What's the worst that could happen if you fail? Can you handle the consequences? If the worst-case scenario is something you can manage or recover from, then the risk might be worth taking. However, if the downside is catastrophic, you may want to reconsider or modify your approach.

3. Create a Backup Plan

Even when taking risks, it's wise to have a backup plan in place. A contingency plan can help you recover more quickly if things don't go as expected. For example, if you're investing a large amount of capital into a new venture, have a plan in place for how you'll pivot or cut losses if the business doesn't perform as projected.

4. Start Small and Scale Up

One way to minimize risk is to start small. Instead of betting everything on one big risk, take smaller steps and scale up as you gain confidence. For instance, if you're launching a new business, test your idea on a smaller scale before expanding. This allows you to gather feedback, make adjustments, and reduce the risk of large-scale failure.

5. Trust Your Gut

While research and planning are critical, there's also an element of intuition in risk-taking. Sometimes, your gut feeling will tell you that a risk is worth taking even when the data isn't perfectly aligned. Trusting your intuition, especially when combined with experience, can help you make bold decisions that lead to success.

Learning from Failure: Turning Setbacks into Success

Failure is not the end of the road—it's a stepping stone to success. Many of the world's most successful people have failed multiple times before achieving greatness. The key is to learn from each failure, make adjustments, and try again with a stronger approach.

Here's how to effectively learn from failure:

1. Analyze What Went Wrong

When you experience a failure, take the time to conduct a post-mortem. What went wrong, and why? Was it a problem with your strategy, timing, or execution? Understanding the root cause of your failure is the first step in preventing it from happening again.

2. Identify What Worked

Even in failure, there are often elements of success. Identify what worked well, and consider how you can build on those strengths. For example, if your marketing campaign didn't bring in as many customers as expected, but your messaging resonated with a small group of people, you might focus on refining your target audience instead of scrapping the entire campaign.

3. Adjust Your Strategy

Once you've analyzed what went wrong and identified what worked, adjust your strategy accordingly. This might involve tweaking your business model, improving your product, or pivoting to a new approach. The goal is to take the lessons you've learned and use them to make your next attempt stronger.

4. Stay Persistent

Perhaps the most important aspect of learning from failure is persistence. Success often requires multiple attempts, and those who give up after their first failure rarely achieve their goals. Stay committed to your vision, keep learning from your mistakes, and continue pushing forward.

Building Resilience Through Risk and Failure

Resilience is the ability to bounce back from adversity and keep moving forward. By embracing risk and failure, you build this critical trait. Resilient people are not immune to setbacks, but they don't let those setbacks stop them. They learn, adapt, and keep going.

Here's how to build resilience:

- **Develop a Strong Support System**: Surround yourself with mentors, peers, and loved ones who can provide guidance and encouragement when you face challenges.
- **Practice Self-Compassion**: Be kind to yourself when things don't go as planned. Acknowledge your efforts, and give yourself credit for taking risks.
- **Maintain a Long-Term Perspective**: Remember that failure is temporary, and success is often the result of perseverance over time.

The Role of Risk in Business and Personal Growth

Risk is an integral part of life, especially in business and personal development. No great achievement comes without a certain level of uncertainty, and embracing risk is often the key to unlocking opportunities that lead to growth and success. While many people shy away from risk, fearing failure or loss, those who learn to assess and embrace it often find themselves on the path to greater accomplishments and personal transformation.

In this chapter, we will explore the role that risk plays in business and personal growth, why taking risks is essential for development, and how to approach risk in a way that maximizes your potential for success while minimizing unnecessary exposure.

Understanding Risk: The Foundation of Growth

Risk is often defined as the possibility of a negative outcome, but it's also a catalyst for positive change. When you step out of your comfort zone to take a chance, you expose yourself to both the possibility of failure and the potential for great rewards. Growth occurs when you navigate this balance and leverage risks to your advantage.

The Two Sides of Risk

There are two main perspectives on risk:

- **Risk as a Threat**: Many people see risk purely in terms of potential loss. In business, this could mean losing money, reputation, or market share. In personal life, it might involve emotional vulnerability, failure, or disappointment.
- **Risk as an Opportunity**: On the other hand, risk can be viewed as an opportunity for growth. Taking a calculated risk can lead to innovation, breakthroughs, and achievements that wouldn't have been possible without stepping into the unknown.

The key to personal and professional growth is learning how to manage risk wisely, recognizing when it's necessary to push forward despite uncertainty, and understanding that calculated risks are often the gateway to success.

Why Risk Is Essential for Business Growth

Business, by its very nature, is a high-risk endeavor. Every entrepreneurial journey starts with a leap of faith, whether it's investing in a new product, expanding into uncharted markets, or adopting innovative technology. Those who succeed in business understand that risk is not something to be avoided—it's something to be embraced strategically.

Here's why risk is crucial for business growth:

1. Innovation Requires Risk

In today's competitive landscape, innovation is the lifeblood of any successful business. However, innovation cannot happen without taking risks. Launching a new product, entering a new market, or developing a disruptive technology all come with a degree of uncertainty. Businesses that remain stagnant in their comfort zones risk being left behind, while those that take calculated risks often become market leaders.

For example, companies like Apple, Tesla, and Amazon have revolutionized their industries by taking bold risks, from investing in new technologies to challenging conventional business models. These risks paid off because the companies were willing to embrace the possibility of failure in exchange for the chance to achieve something extraordinary.

2. Growth Requires Investment

Every major business growth opportunity involves some level of risk, particularly financial risk. Whether you're hiring new employees, expanding operations, or investing in marketing, each decision requires a commitment of resources with no guaranteed return. However, without taking these risks, a business cannot grow.

Consider the case of startups, where entrepreneurs often invest their savings or take on significant loans to fund their ventures. The risk of failure is high, but so is the potential for success. Those who carefully assess and manage their risks often find themselves building companies that generate significant returns.

3. Competitive Advantage Through Risk

Businesses that take strategic risks often gain a competitive advantage. While others may hesitate to act, risk-takers capitalize on emerging trends, new technologies, and untapped markets. By being the first mover or adopting innovative practices, companies can establish themselves as leaders, setting the pace for others to follow.

Take Uber as an example. When Uber launched its ride-hailing service, the concept of using an app to summon rides was new, and the company faced significant regulatory and market risks.

However, Uber's willingness to take those risks gave it a massive first-mover advantage, disrupting the traditional taxi industry and becoming a household name globally.

Why Risk Is Essential for Personal Growth

In addition to business, risk is crucial for personal growth. Personal development requires stepping out of your comfort zone, challenging yourself, and confronting the fear of failure. Whether it's pursuing a new career, developing a new skill, or making a significant life decision, personal growth often involves risk.

1. Stepping Outside Your Comfort Zone

One of the most significant barriers to personal growth is staying in your comfort zone. When you stick with what is familiar and safe, you limit your potential for improvement. Risk forces you to stretch your capabilities, learn new things, and expand your horizons.

For example, if you're considering changing careers, the risk of starting over might be daunting. However, the potential rewards—greater job satisfaction, higher income, and personal fulfillment—often make the risk worth taking. Growth comes from pushing yourself to try new things and face new challenges.

2. Overcoming Fear of Failure

Fear of failure is one of the most common reasons people avoid taking risks. However, failure is often a necessary step on the path to success. Personal growth comes from learning how to handle setbacks, adapt to changing circumstances, and persevere in the face of challenges.

Failure teaches resilience, a key component of personal development. By facing risks and potential failures head-on, you build the mental toughness required to handle life's inevitable challenges. The more risks you take, the more comfortable you become with uncertainty, and the better you learn to cope with failure.

3. Building Confidence Through Risk-Taking

Taking risks and succeeding—whether in business or personal endeavors—boosts self-confidence. Each time you take a leap of faith and see positive results, you develop greater belief in your abilities. Confidence is built through action, and action requires risk.

For example, if you take the risk of speaking in public for the first time and succeed, your confidence in your communication skills will grow. This newfound confidence can lead to more opportunities, whether in business networking, leadership, or personal relationships.

4. Risk Leads to Personal Transformation

Big life changes—moving to a new city, starting a family, or pursuing a dream—require significant risks. Yet, these are often the moments that lead to profound personal transformation. By taking risks, you expose yourself to new experiences, challenges, and opportunities that shape who you are and help you grow.

The risk of failure or uncertainty is a small price to pay for the personal growth that comes from embracing change. Each step outside your comfort zone brings you closer to realizing your full potential.

Approaching Risk Strategically: How to Minimize Downside and Maximize Upside

While risk is essential for growth, not all risks are created equal. The key to using risk as a tool for success is to approach it strategically, with a focus on minimizing downside and maximizing upside.

Here are some strategies for managing risk effectively:

1. Assess the Potential Rewards

Before taking any significant risk, ask yourself, "What's the potential upside?" If the reward is worth the potential downside, the risk might be worth taking. This applies in both business and personal life. For example, if you're considering launching a new product, think about the potential market size, profitability, and long-term impact.

2. Consider the Worst-Case Scenario

It's important to weigh the worst-case scenario before making a decision. Can you handle the consequences if the risk doesn't pay off? If the potential loss is manageable, you might decide that the risk is worth taking. However, if the downside is too significant, you might need to reconsider or find ways to mitigate the risk.

3. Take Calculated Risks

A calculated risk is one where you have done your research and considered all factors before making a decision. It's not a blind leap of faith; it's an informed choice. To take calculated risks, gather as much information as possible, consult experts if necessary, and weigh the pros and cons carefully.

4. Diversify Your Risk

In business, diversification is a key strategy for managing risk. Instead of putting all your resources into one venture or idea, spread them across multiple opportunities. This way, if one risk doesn't pay off, you still have other ventures that may succeed.

5. Develop a Contingency Plan

When taking a risk, always have a backup plan. What will you do if things don't go as expected? A contingency plan allows you to act quickly and minimize losses if the risk doesn't work out as planned.

6. Learn to Trust Your Intuition

While data and research are essential, there's also a place for intuition in risk-taking. Over time, as you gain experience, you develop a gut feeling about certain risks. Learning to trust your instincts, especially when combined with data, can lead to wise risk-taking.

Learning from Failure and Developing Resilience

Failure is often seen as something to be avoided at all costs, but in reality, it is one of the most powerful teachers in both business and personal life. It offers lessons that success often cannot, and it plays a crucial role in building resilience—the ability to recover from setbacks and keep moving forward. Those who succeed in the long run are not those who never fail, but those who learn from their failures and use them as stepping stones toward growth.

In this chapter, we will explore the importance of failure as a learning tool, how to reframe failure as an opportunity, and the ways in which developing resilience can transform setbacks into success. We will also discuss practical strategies for bouncing back from failure and growing stronger as a result.

The Hidden Value of Failure

Failure is frequently misunderstood. Society often portrays it as a negative experience that should be feared and avoided. However, failure is essential for growth, innovation, and success. The most successful entrepreneurs, leaders, and innovators have all experienced failures, but what sets them apart is their ability to extract value from those experiences and apply what they've learned moving forward.

Why Failure Is a Powerful Teacher

1. **Failure Reveals Weaknesses**: Failure exposes the areas where improvement is needed. When you fail, it forces you to confront shortcomings in your strategy, skills, or approach. While this can be uncomfortable, it is the first step toward growth. Without failure, you may never become aware of these gaps.
2. **Failure Encourages Innovation**: When something doesn't work, it pushes you to think creatively about how to approach the problem differently. Many of the most groundbreaking inventions and ideas came from people who tried, failed, and then innovated based on their failures.
3. **Failure Builds Character**: Facing failure head-on and choosing to persevere builds qualities like humility, patience, and grit. These qualities are invaluable, not only in business but in life. They equip you to handle future challenges with greater confidence and wisdom.
4. **Failure Fuels Motivation**: For many people, failure can spark a desire to prove themselves, prompting them to work harder and smarter. While success can lead to complacency, failure can reignite your passion and determination to achieve your goals.

Reframing Failure: Turning Setbacks into Opportunities

A critical step in learning from failure is changing the way you perceive it. Rather than viewing failure as a dead-end, it's essential to see it as part of the process of growth. This shift in perspective can transform the way you approach challenges and setbacks.

1. View Failure as Feedback, Not Finality

Failure is not an endpoint—it's feedback. When something doesn't work out, it's simply a signal that adjustments are needed. Rather than interpreting failure as a reflection of your worth or abilities, see it as valuable information that can guide you toward success.

For instance, when a product launch fails or a business deal falls through, instead of feeling defeated, analyze the situation. What didn't work? Was it a marketing misstep, a product flaw, or poor timing? By treating failure as feedback, you can refine your approach and increase your chances of success the next time around.

2. Embrace a Growth Mindset

Adopting a growth mindset—a concept developed by psychologist Carol Dweck—is essential for turning failure into a learning experience. A growth mindset is the belief that abilities and intelligence can be developed through effort, learning, and persistence.

People with a growth mindset view failure as an opportunity to learn and grow, whereas those with a fixed mindset see failure as a reflection of their inherent abilities. By cultivating a growth mindset, you'll approach failure with curiosity, eager to learn from it rather than fearing it.

3. Detach from the Fear of Failure

One of the biggest barriers to success is the fear of failure. This fear can prevent you from taking risks, trying new things, and pursuing ambitious goals. The truth is, failure is an inevitable part of any journey toward success, and the more you fear it, the less likely you are to push beyond your limits.

To overcome this fear, it's helpful to acknowledge that failure is a normal part of life and business. Everyone fails at some point, and failure doesn't define you—it's how you respond to it that matters.

Developing Resilience: The Key to Bouncing Back Stronger

Resilience is the ability to recover from setbacks and continue moving forward, even when things don't go as planned. It's what separates those who give up after failure from those who keep trying until they succeed. Resilience is not something you're born with—it's a skill that can be developed through experience and intentional practice.

Why Resilience Matters

- **Resilience Keeps You Moving Forward**: In both business and life, there will always be challenges and obstacles. Resilience enables you to keep going when others would give up. It helps you maintain focus on your long-term goals, even in the face of temporary setbacks.
- **Resilience Helps You Adapt to Change**: Change is inevitable, and those who are resilient can adapt quickly. They are flexible and open to new approaches, which allows them to thrive in uncertain environments.
- **Resilience Builds Confidence**: Every time you bounce back from a setback, you reinforce your belief in your ability to handle adversity. This builds confidence,

which is crucial for taking on bigger challenges and risks in the future.

How to Build Resilience

1. **Accept That Failure Is Part of the Process**

The first step in building resilience is accepting that failure is a natural and inevitable part of the growth process. It doesn't mean that you're inadequate or that your efforts are in vain. Once you accept that failure is a normal part of the journey, it becomes easier to handle and learn from it.

2. **Practice Self-Compassion**

After a failure, it's important to be kind to yourself. Self-compassion means treating yourself with the same understanding and encouragement that you would offer a friend who is going through a tough time. Rather than beating yourself up for mistakes, recognize that failure is a learning opportunity, and give yourself credit for trying.

3. **Focus on What You Can Control**

When faced with failure, it's easy to feel overwhelmed by all the factors that contributed to the setback. However, not everything is within your control. Instead of dwelling on things you can't change, focus on the aspects you can influence. This might involve improving your skills, adjusting your strategy, or seeking new opportunities.

4. **Learn from Every Setback**

Resilience isn't just about bouncing back—it's about bouncing back better. Each failure is an opportunity to learn something new, whether it's about yourself, your business, or the market.

Conduct a thorough post-mortem after every failure to identify the lessons you can take away and apply to future endeavors.

For example, if a business venture fails, reflect on what went wrong. Did you misjudge the market demand? Did you overlook a key financial aspect? By understanding the reasons for your failure, you can avoid making the same mistakes again.

5. **Build a Support System**

Resilience doesn't mean going it alone. Surround yourself with a support system of friends, family, mentors, or colleagues who can provide guidance, encouragement, and perspective when you encounter setbacks. A strong support network can help you regain confidence and motivation when things get tough.

6. **Set Small, Achievable Goals**

One way to build resilience is by setting small, incremental goals that move you toward your larger objectives. These small wins help build momentum and boost your confidence, making it easier to recover from bigger failures. Each step forward reinforces the belief that progress is possible, even in the face of adversity.

Learning from Failure: A Step-by-Step Process

When failure strikes, the way you respond to it will determine how quickly and effectively you can bounce back. Here's a step-by-step process to help you learn from failure and use it as a foundation for future success:

1. Acknowledge the Failure

The first step is to acknowledge what happened. Avoid the temptation to ignore or downplay the failure. By confronting it directly, you take ownership of the situation, which empowers you to take control of your response.

2. Take Responsibility

It's important to take responsibility for your role in the failure, but avoid blaming yourself excessively. Instead of seeing failure as a personal flaw, view it as a result of specific decisions, actions, or circumstances. This shift in perspective helps you focus on practical solutions rather than self-criticism.

3. Analyze the Situation

Conduct a thorough analysis of what went wrong. Break down the failure into its component parts: What decisions led to this outcome? Were there warning signs you missed? Did external factors play a role? This analysis will provide valuable insights that can guide your future actions.

4. Extract the Lessons

Once you've analyzed the situation, extract the lessons. What can you learn from this experience? How can you apply those lessons moving forward? This might involve refining your strategy, improving your skills, or adjusting your goals. The key is to treat each failure as a learning experience that brings you closer to success.

5. Adjust and Move Forward

After extracting the lessons, it's time to adjust your approach. Use the insights gained from your failure to make smarter decisions in the future. Then, move forward with confidence, knowing that failure has made you stronger and more prepared for the challenges ahead.

Chapter 4: Strategic Thinking

In the business world, there are thinkers and there are doers. But those who succeed at the highest levels master the art of strategic thinking. Strategic thinking isn't just about setting goals or making plans; it's about developing a mindset that allows you to view the business landscape from a high vantage point, to see the bigger picture, and to make decisions that align with long-term success.

In this chapter, we will dive deep into what strategic thinking really means, why it's crucial for business success, and how you can cultivate this critical skill.

What is Strategic Thinking?

Strategic thinking is the ability to foresee future challenges and opportunities, assess available resources, and develop a plan that ensures long-term success. It's about being proactive, not just reactive. While tactical thinking is concerned with short-term actions and solving immediate problems, strategic thinking focuses on the long game.

To be a strategic thinker means that you consistently ask yourself questions such as:

- What are the current trends in my industry, and how can I position my business to take advantage of them?
- What potential risks could disrupt my business, and how can I mitigate them?
- How will my decisions today impact my business five, ten, or twenty years down the line?

Why Strategic Thinking is Important

The importance of strategic thinking in business cannot be overstated. Without it, businesses often fall into the trap of focusing solely on short-term gains, which can lead to burnout, stagnation, or failure. On the other hand, strategic thinking helps you anticipate changes in the market, avoid costly mistakes, and innovate ahead of your competition.

1. Anticipating Market Changes

Markets are constantly evolving due to technology, consumer behavior, economic shifts, and regulations. Strategic thinking allows you to stay ahead of these changes. For instance, companies like Netflix and Apple succeeded because they didn't just follow current trends—they anticipated future ones. While their competitors were caught off guard by digital streaming or technological advancements, these companies saw the future and adapted.

2. Maximizing Resources

Strategic thinking helps you allocate resources—time, money, talent—more effectively. Instead of spending on every opportunity that presents itself, you learn to focus your efforts where they will have the greatest long-term impact. You begin to prioritize quality over quantity, understanding that not every idea or project is worth pursuing.

3. Making Informed Decisions

Every day, business leaders face a barrage of decisions, from hiring new employees to launching new products. Strategic thinking sharpens your decision-making process. Instead of reacting impulsively to every situation, you learn to evaluate decisions based on your long-term vision, ensuring that every action taken is a step toward achieving your overall goals.

4. Building a Sustainable Business

In the world of business, it's easy to get caught up in the chase for immediate profits, but long-term success requires a sustainable approach. Strategic thinkers build businesses that last. They don't just seek to capitalize on current opportunities but invest in building a brand, a team, and a product that can weather the storms of competition and changing market conditions.

How to Develop Strategic Thinking

Strategic thinking is not an innate talent; it's a skill that can be developed and honed over time. Here are key steps to cultivating a strategic mindset:

1. Think Long-Term

Start by shifting your perspective from short-term problem-solving to long-term planning. Where do you want your business to be in five years? What about ten or twenty years? By keeping the long-term in mind, you ensure that the actions you take today contribute to future success.

2. Analyze and Reflect

A good strategist is an avid learner. You need to constantly evaluate what is working and what isn't. Take time to analyze your business decisions and the outcomes they produce. What could you have done differently? How can you improve moving forward? This process of reflection helps you identify patterns and develop a deeper understanding of your business.

3. Stay Informed

To think strategically, you must have a solid understanding of your industry, market trends, competitors, and emerging technologies. Make it a habit to read industry reports, attend conferences, and engage with thought leaders. The more information you have, the better equipped you will be to make informed decisions that position your business for long-term success.

4. Ask "What If?"

Strategic thinkers constantly challenge the status quo by asking "What if?" questions. What if a competitor releases a new product tomorrow? What if your supply chain is disrupted? What if your target market's preferences change? This type of thinking allows you to anticipate challenges and develop contingency plans to address them before they arise.

5. Collaborate and Seek Diverse Opinions

Strategic thinking is not done in isolation. Involving your team in brainstorming sessions or seeking advice from mentors and industry experts can provide valuable insights that you might not have considered on your own. Diversity of thought helps you approach problems from multiple angles and create more comprehensive strategies.

6. Embrace Flexibility

Strategic thinkers are adaptable. While you should have a clear vision of where you want your business to go, it's important to remain flexible enough to change course when necessary. If new information presents itself, or if market conditions change, don't be afraid to pivot. The ability to adjust your strategy on the fly can often mean the difference between success and failure.

Strategic Thinking in Action: Real-World Examples

1. Amazon's Relentless Innovation

Amazon's founder, Jeff Bezos, exemplifies strategic thinking in action. From the beginning, Bezos envisioned Amazon not just as an online bookstore, but as a tech-driven company that could dominate e-commerce. By strategically investing in new technologies and expanding Amazon's offerings, Bezos created a business empire that now spans cloud computing, artificial intelligence, logistics, and entertainment. His long-term vision, coupled with the flexibility to adapt to changing market conditions, has made Amazon one of the most successful companies in the world.

2. Tesla's Bet on the Future

Elon Musk, the CEO of Tesla, is another example of a strategic thinker who has bet on the future. Musk saw the potential for electric vehicles long before they were popular, investing heavily in technology and infrastructure to position Tesla as a market leader. Despite early skepticism, his commitment to a long-term vision has made Tesla one of the most valuable automotive companies in the world.

Developing a Strategic Approach to Decision-Making

In the fast-paced world of business, decisions must often be made quickly, but speed without strategy can lead to costly mistakes. Developing a strategic approach to decision-making is about balancing the need for quick action with thoughtful, long-term planning. It requires a framework that allows you to evaluate options, anticipate potential outcomes, and align decisions with your broader goals. In this sub-chapter, we will explore how to craft a strategic approach to decision-making, ensuring that every choice you make is informed, deliberate, and effective.

The Importance of Strategic Decision-Making

Decision-making is one of the most critical functions of leadership. Whether you're a business owner, manager, or entrepreneur, the decisions you make shape the future of your organization. While some decisions seem insignificant in the moment, they often have long-term consequences. A strategic approach to decision-making ensures that you consider both immediate needs and future implications.

1. Aligning Decisions with Long-Term Goals

At the core of strategic decision-making is the alignment of each choice with your long-term business objectives. Every decision, whether it's hiring a new employee, launching a product, or entering a new market, should move your business closer to its goals. Without this alignment, decisions become reactive and fragmented, leading to inefficiencies and missed opportunities.

For example, if your goal is to expand your business globally within the next five years, decisions about partnerships, product development, and talent acquisition should all be evaluated in light of how they contribute to this long-term vision. Strategic decision-making ensures that even small, day-to-day choices are made with an eye toward the future.

2. Anticipating Future Challenges and Opportunities

Strategic decision-makers think beyond the present. They anticipate future challenges and opportunities by constantly monitoring industry trends, technological advancements, and shifts in consumer behavior. This forward-thinking approach helps you make decisions that not only solve immediate problems but also prepare your business for what's to come.

Take, for example, the rise of e-commerce. Companies that anticipated this shift early on were able to position themselves for success, while those that failed to recognize the trend struggled to catch up. A strategic approach to decision-making allows you to stay ahead of the curve, making proactive choices that position your business for long-term growth.

3. Managing Risks

Risk is an inherent part of business, but strategic decision-making helps mitigate unnecessary risks. By considering the potential outcomes of each decision, you can weigh the risks against the rewards and make more informed choices. Strategic thinkers understand that not every decision will lead to immediate success, but by calculating risks carefully, they minimize the chance of failure.

One key element of strategic decision-making is having contingency plans. When you're aware of potential risks, you can develop strategies to navigate or avoid them. This doesn't mean being overly cautious but rather making informed decisions that allow your business to thrive even in uncertain circumstances.

Steps to Developing a Strategic Approach to Decision-Making

Developing a strategic approach to decision-making doesn't happen overnight, but by following these steps, you can build a framework that enables better, more strategic choices.

1. Define Your Long-Term Vision and Goals

The first step in strategic decision-making is having a clear understanding of your long-term business vision and goals. What are you aiming to achieve in the next five, ten, or twenty years? Whether it's expanding into new markets, increasing revenue, or becoming a leader in innovation, your decisions should consistently reflect and support these goals.

Without a clear vision, it's easy to get sidetracked by short-term wins or distractions. Strategic decision-makers always ask themselves: "How does this decision bring us closer to our goals?" If a decision doesn't align with your long-term vision, it's often better to reconsider or refine it.

2. Gather and Analyze Information

Strategic decision-making is grounded in data. Before making any significant decision, take the time to gather and analyze relevant information. This might include market research, customer feedback, financial reports, competitor analysis, or trends in technology. The more informed you are, the better your decisions will be.

For instance, if you're deciding whether to introduce a new product, you should first analyze market demand, customer preferences, and competitor offerings. This will help you make a decision based on facts rather than assumptions or gut feelings. Data-driven decisions are far more likely to lead to success.

3. Evaluate Options and Alternatives

In strategic decision-making, rarely is there only one clear path. After gathering information, evaluate all potential options and consider their pros and cons. Sometimes, the best decision is not the most obvious one, and exploring alternatives can reveal more innovative or effective solutions.

To make this process easier, consider using tools such as SWOT analysis (Strengths, Weaknesses, Opportunities, Threats) or decision matrices, which help break down complex choices into manageable factors. By thoroughly evaluating each option, you ensure that the decision you make is well thought out and aligned with your goals.

4. Consider Short-Term and Long-Term Impacts

One of the key principles of strategic decision-making is balancing short-term needs with long-term goals. While some decisions might offer immediate benefits, they could undermine your long-term success. Conversely, decisions that seem difficult or resource-intensive in the short term may lead to substantial long-term gains.

For example, investing in cutting-edge technology might be expensive initially, but it could significantly increase efficiency and competitiveness in the long run. Strategic decision-makers carefully weigh these trade-offs, ensuring that short-term actions support long-term growth.

5. Involve Key Stakeholders

Strategic decision-making isn't a solo endeavor. Involving key stakeholders—whether it's your leadership team, employees, customers, or external advisors—provides diverse perspectives and insights that you might not have considered. Collaborative decision-making often leads to more well-rounded and effective solutions.

When seeking input, ensure that those involved understand the long-term goals and objectives. This ensures that their feedback aligns with the broader strategy. By engaging stakeholders early in the decision-making process, you also build consensus and increase the likelihood of successful implementation.

6. Be Adaptable and Open to Change

The business landscape is constantly evolving, and strategic decision-makers must be adaptable. While having a plan is essential, it's equally important to remain flexible. Sometimes, new information will emerge that challenges your initial assumptions or reveals a better course of action.

Being adaptable doesn't mean being indecisive. It means being open to change when necessary and adjusting your decisions based on new data or circumstances. The best strategists are those who can pivot when needed without losing sight of the long-term vision.

7. Implement and Monitor the Decision

Once a decision is made, the next step is implementation. Strategic decision-making doesn't stop at choosing the right course of action—it extends to ensuring that the decision is executed effectively. Develop an implementation plan, set clear timelines, and assign responsibilities to ensure accountability.

After implementation, it's important to monitor the results. Regularly reviewing the impact of your decisions allows you to identify whether the desired outcomes are being achieved. If not, be prepared to adjust your strategy. This continuous feedback loop is a key component of strategic decision-making, allowing for ongoing refinement and improvement.

Overcoming Common Challenges in Strategic Decision-Making

While strategic decision-making is essential for long-term success, it's not without its challenges. Here are some common obstacles and how to overcome them:

1. Analysis Paralysis

Gathering data and evaluating options are crucial, but too much information can lead to analysis paralysis, where decision-makers become overwhelmed and unable to make a choice. To avoid this, set clear deadlines for decision-making, and focus on the most relevant information. Remember, no decision will ever be 100% risk-free, but delaying too long can result in missed opportunities.

2. Short-Term Pressures

In business, there's often pressure to make decisions that yield immediate results, particularly from investors or stakeholders. While short-term wins are important, always consider how these decisions impact the long-term trajectory of your business. Striking a balance between short-term and long-term thinking is key to making sustainable decisions.

3. Uncertainty and Risk

All decisions carry some degree of uncertainty, but strategic thinkers embrace calculated risks. By thoroughly evaluating potential risks and developing contingency plans, you can make informed decisions even in uncertain conditions.

Tools for Strategic Planning: SWOT Analysis and Competitive Analysis

Strategic planning is essential for setting the direction of any business. It helps leaders define their goals, allocate resources effectively, and navigate the competitive landscape. To plan strategically, businesses must use proven tools that provide insights into their internal strengths and weaknesses, as well as the opportunities and threats in the external environment. Two of the most effective tools for strategic planning are **SWOT analysis** and **competitive analysis**.

In this sub-chapter, we'll explore how these tools work, how to apply them effectively, and why they are crucial for making informed business decisions.

1. SWOT Analysis: Understanding Your Internal and External Environment

SWOT analysis is one of the most widely used tools in strategic planning. The acronym stands for **Strengths, Weaknesses, Opportunities, and Threats**. This framework helps businesses assess both internal and external factors that affect their success.

It is simple to understand yet powerful in its ability to provide clear, actionable insights.

A. Strengths

Strengths are the internal attributes of a business that give it an advantage over competitors. These could be unique resources, capabilities, or any factors that contribute to success. When conducting a SWOT analysis, you should ask yourself:

- What does your company do better than others?
- What resources or assets do you possess that your competitors don't?
- What are the key areas where your business excels (e.g., customer service, innovation, branding)?

Identifying your strengths allows you to capitalize on them, making sure they remain at the core of your strategy. For example, if your company has a strong brand identity, this strength can be leveraged in marketing campaigns to differentiate your products from competitors.

B. Weaknesses

Weaknesses are internal factors that hinder your business from achieving its full potential. These could be limitations in resources, skills, or areas where your competitors outperform you. To identify your weaknesses, consider questions like:

- What processes or systems need improvement?
- Where are you losing market share to competitors?
- What areas of your business lack efficiency or innovation?

Acknowledging weaknesses is critical to strategic planning, as it helps you address internal issues before they become larger problems. For instance, if your customer service is subpar compared to your competitors, it might be time to invest in training or new technologies to enhance the customer experience.

C. Opportunities

Opportunities refer to external factors that could benefit your business if you act on them. These could be changes in market trends, technological advancements, or regulatory shifts. When identifying opportunities, ask:

- What emerging trends can you capitalize on?
- Are there any gaps in the market that you could fill?
- How can you leverage technology or partnerships to enhance your business?

Opportunities often arise from changes in the market, and strategic businesses position themselves to take advantage of these shifts. For example, the increasing demand for eco-friendly products has opened opportunities for businesses to innovate and meet consumer needs in the sustainability space.

D. Threats

Threats are external factors that pose risks to your business. These could include new competitors, changes in regulations, economic downturns, or shifts in consumer behavior. To assess threats, consider the following:

- Who are your current and potential competitors, and how do they threaten your market share?
- Are there regulatory changes or economic factors that could disrupt your industry?
- How might changes in consumer preferences impact your products or services?

Identifying threats helps you create strategies to mitigate risks. For instance, if a new competitor is entering your market with a lower-priced product, you might need to focus on strengthening your brand's value proposition or reducing costs to remain competitive.

Conducting a SWOT Analysis

To conduct a successful SWOT analysis:

1. Gather key stakeholders from different areas of your business (e.g., marketing, finance, operations) to get diverse perspectives.
2. Begin by brainstorming each quadrant (Strengths, Weaknesses, Opportunities, and Threats).
3. Prioritize the most important factors in each category.
4. Use the insights gained to craft strategies that build on strengths, address weaknesses, seize opportunities, and mitigate threats.

2. Competitive Analysis: Navigating the Competitive Landscape

While SWOT analysis helps you understand your internal and external environment, **competitive analysis** focuses specifically on understanding your competitors. It's a crucial tool for determining how your business stacks up against others in the market and identifying opportunities to gain a competitive edge.

A. Identifying Competitors

Before diving into competitive analysis, the first step is to identify who your competitors are. These can be:

- **Direct competitors**: Companies that offer the same or very similar products or services.
- **Indirect competitors**: Businesses that offer different products or services but target the same customer base.

- **Potential competitors**: Companies that might enter your market in the future.

For example, if you're running a clothing brand, your direct competitors would be other fashion brands targeting your market segment, while indirect competitors might include lifestyle brands or companies that offer accessories or footwear that appeal to the same audience.

B. Assessing Competitor Strategies

Once you've identified your competitors, the next step is to assess their strategies. This includes understanding their:

- **Product offerings**: What products or services do they offer, and how do they compare to yours in terms of quality, price, and features?
- **Marketing and branding**: How do they position themselves in the market? What messaging and branding tactics do they use to appeal to their target audience?
- **Customer experience**: How do they interact with customers? What is their approach to customer service, loyalty programs, and user experience?

By assessing these areas, you can identify what your competitors are doing well and where they may be falling short. For example, if a competitor has a strong digital marketing presence, you may need to invest more in online advertising or content marketing to stay competitive.

C. Analyzing Market Positioning

Market positioning refers to how your competitors are perceived by customers. Are they seen as high-end or budget-friendly? Do they cater to niche markets or a broad audience? Understanding how competitors are positioned helps you find gaps in the market where you can differentiate your business.

For instance, if all your competitors are focusing on affordability, there might be an opportunity for you to position your brand as a premium option. By offering superior quality, customer service, or innovative features, you can capture a different segment of the market.

D. Evaluating Competitor Performance

Competitor performance can be evaluated using several key indicators, including:

- **Market share**: How much of the market do they control? Are they gaining or losing ground?
- **Financial health**: Are they profitable? What is their revenue growth rate?
- **Customer satisfaction**: What do customers think of their products or services? Do they have high customer retention rates or a lot of complaints?

By regularly tracking these performance indicators, you can identify trends that signal opportunities or threats. For example, if a competitor is gaining significant market share, you may need to adjust your pricing, distribution, or promotional strategies to maintain your competitive position.

E. Competitive Analysis Tools

There are several tools available to help you conduct a thorough competitive analysis:

- **Porter's Five Forces**: This model helps assess the competitive forces that shape your industry, including the threat of new entrants, the bargaining power of suppliers and buyers, and the intensity of competitive rivalry.
- **Benchmarking**: This process involves comparing your business performance against competitors in specific areas, such as cost efficiency, product quality, or customer service.

- **Market share analysis**: By tracking market share data over time, you can see how your business compares to competitors and identify growth opportunities.

Combining SWOT Analysis and Competitive Analysis for Strategic Planning

When used together, SWOT analysis and competitive analysis provide a comprehensive view of your business environment. SWOT analysis helps you assess internal and external factors affecting your business, while competitive analysis gives you insight into how you measure up against competitors. By combining the insights from both tools, you can craft more effective strategic plans.

For example:

- **Strengths** from your SWOT analysis can help you identify areas where you already outperform competitors and build on them.
- **Weaknesses** can highlight internal improvements needed to compete more effectively.
- **Opportunities** identified through both analyses can help you spot new market trends or gaps that your competitors haven't yet exploited.
- **Threats** identified in your SWOT analysis can be mitigated by understanding your competitors' strategies and finding ways to counteract them.

Chapter 5: Networking and Relationship Building

In the world of business, success is rarely achieved in isolation. The people you meet and the relationships you cultivate are often as important as the strategies you develop or the products you sell. Networking and relationship building are essential skills that open doors to opportunities, create partnerships, and build the trust necessary for long-term business success.

This chapter will dive deep into the significance of networking and relationship building, exploring both traditional methods and modern approaches. Whether you're an entrepreneur, a business professional, or someone looking to build their personal brand, mastering the art of networking is critical.

Why Networking Matters

Networking is the process of creating and nurturing professional relationships that are mutually beneficial. It goes beyond exchanging business cards or adding contacts on LinkedIn—it's about forming meaningful connections that provide value for both parties. Here's why networking is crucial in business:

1. **Access to Opportunities:** One of the biggest benefits of networking is access to opportunities. Whether it's a job offer, a potential partnership, or a new client, networking opens the door to new ventures. Many opportunities are never publicly advertised and are shared within networks through referrals.
2. **Building Your Reputation:** Your network can help build your personal and professional reputation. When you consistently provide value to others, people are more likely to refer you to their contacts. Word of mouth and recommendations are powerful tools in building credibility.

3. **Knowledge Sharing and Learning:** Networking exposes you to new ideas, trends, and industry knowledge. By engaging with professionals in your field, you can learn from their experiences and share insights that can benefit your own business.
4. **Support System:** Networking provides a valuable support system. Being able to turn to trusted contacts for advice, mentorship, or support during difficult times can be invaluable. Strong relationships built on trust and respect are the backbone of a reliable support network.

The Foundations of Effective Networking

To be successful at networking, you need more than just a willingness to meet new people. Effective networking requires a strategy and a commitment to building long-term relationships. Here are the key principles for building a strong network:

1. Give Before You Get

Successful networking isn't about asking for favors or expecting something in return. Instead, it's about offering value to others first. Think about what you can provide, whether it's sharing useful information, offering to connect someone with a contact, or providing advice. The more value you provide, the more likely others will reciprocate when you need help.

2. Be Authentic

Authenticity is critical in building trust. People can tell when someone is networking for purely self-serving reasons. Authenticity comes from a genuine interest in the other person's work, challenges, and successes. Approach networking with a mindset of curiosity and empathy, and be sincere in your interactions.

3. Quality Over Quantity

It's easy to get caught up in the idea that having a large network is the key to success, but quality is more important than quantity. A few meaningful relationships can have far greater impact than a long list of contacts with whom you have no real connection. Focus on building deep relationships with people who share your values and goals.

4. Follow Up Consistently

Building a network isn't a one-time event; it requires consistent effort over time. After meeting someone, make sure to follow up and stay in touch. Whether it's through email, social media, or attending the same events, maintaining regular contact shows that you're invested in the relationship.

5. Be a Good Listener

Networking isn't just about talking about yourself—it's about listening to others. By being an attentive listener, you show respect for the other person's opinions and experiences. People are more likely to remember you and want to engage with you if they feel heard and understood.

Modern Networking: The Power of Digital Tools

While traditional face-to-face networking remains important, digital tools have transformed the way people connect and build relationships. Platforms like LinkedIn, Twitter, and even industry-specific forums allow you to connect with professionals from all over the world. Here's how to leverage digital tools for effective networking:

1. LinkedIn: Your Digital Business Card

LinkedIn is the world's largest professional network, and it's an essential tool for modern networking. Your LinkedIn profile is your digital business card, and it should represent you in the best possible light. Here's how to optimize your LinkedIn presence:

- **Profile Picture and Headline:** Use a professional headshot and write a clear headline that reflects your expertise and what you do. Make it compelling and specific.
- **Summary and Experience:** Write a concise and engaging summary that showcases your skills, accomplishments, and what you can offer. Your experience should be detailed enough to show your professional journey but concise to maintain the reader's interest.
- **Engage with Others:** Comment on posts, share industry insights, and actively engage with your network. The more you contribute, the more visible and valuable you become within your network.

2. Twitter: Networking in Real Time

Twitter is a powerful tool for real-time engagement, allowing you to participate in industry conversations and connect with thought leaders. Follow industry hashtags, engage with experts, and share your thoughts on relevant topics. Twitter chats—organized discussions around specific topics—are a great way to meet like-minded professionals.

3. Online Communities and Forums

Industry-specific communities and forums, such as Reddit threads, Facebook groups, or platforms like Slack and Discord, provide spaces for professionals to share ideas, ask questions, and network. These platforms allow you to build relationships within your industry and establish yourself as an expert by contributing valuable insights.

4. Personal Branding Through Content Creation

One of the most effective ways to network in the digital age is by creating and sharing content. Writing blog posts, creating videos, or sharing insights on platforms like Medium, LinkedIn, or YouTube allows you to demonstrate your expertise and attract like-minded professionals. When others find value in your content, they are more likely to reach out and connect with you.

Building Strong, Long-Lasting Relationships

Networking is the first step, but maintaining and deepening relationships is the key to long-term success. Here's how to build relationships that last:

1. Follow Up with Gratitude

After meeting someone, follow up with a thank-you note or message. Express gratitude for their time and acknowledge any value they provided during your conversation. This small gesture sets the tone for a positive relationship moving forward.

2. Stay in Touch Regularly

Don't let months or years go by without reaching out to your contacts. A quick message or phone call to check in, share news, or offer help keeps the relationship active. If you wait too long, your connection may fade, and rekindling it can be challenging.

3. Offer Help Without Being Asked

If you come across information or an opportunity that could benefit someone in your network, share it without waiting for them to ask. This proactive approach demonstrates that you are genuinely invested in the success of others, which builds trust and strengthens relationships.

4. Personalize Your Interactions

Whenever possible, personalize your interactions with people in your network. Mention specific things you discussed in previous conversations or refer to something relevant to their interests. This shows that you're paying attention and value the relationship beyond surface-level engagement.

5. Be Consistent and Reliable

Consistency is crucial in maintaining relationships. If you commit to helping someone or following up on a discussion, do it in a timely manner. People appreciate reliability, and being dependable is a key part of building a strong reputation in your network.

The Role of Mentorship in Networking

One of the most valuable aspects of networking is the opportunity to find mentors and be a mentor to others. Mentorship is a relationship in which a more experienced person guides and supports a less experienced individual. Here's why mentorship is important and how to build mentor-mentee relationships:

1. Finding a Mentor

A mentor can provide invaluable guidance, helping you navigate challenges, develop new skills, and make informed decisions. To find a mentor, look for someone whose career path or expertise aligns with your goals. You can connect with potential mentors through networking events, professional organizations, or even within your workplace.

When approaching a potential mentor, be respectful of their time and show a genuine interest in learning from them. Mentorship is built on mutual respect, and mentors are often more willing to invest time in someone who demonstrates a strong desire for growth.

2. Becoming a Mentor

As you advance in your career, you'll have opportunities to mentor others. Being a mentor not only allows you to give back but also helps you refine your own leadership skills. When mentoring someone, focus on listening to their challenges, offering guidance without dictating, and supporting their growth.

Networking Etiquette: Dos and Don'ts

Networking, whether in person or online, requires a level of professionalism and etiquette. Here are some key dos and don'ts to keep in mind:

Do:

- **Be polite and respectful:** Treat everyone you meet with respect, regardless of their position or perceived influence.
- **Be prepared:** Have a clear understanding of your goals and what you can offer before entering networking situations.
- **Follow up promptly:** After meeting someone, follow up within a few days to maintain the momentum of the connection.
- **Be punctual:** Whether it's an in-person meeting or a virtual one, punctuality shows respect for the other person's time.

Don't:

- **Be overly aggressive:** Networking is about building relationships, not hard-selling yourself or your business.
- **Ask for too much too soon:** Don't immediately ask for favors or opportunities before establishing trust and rapport.
- **Forget to listen:** Effective networking is as much about listening as it is about talking. Don't dominate the conversation.
- **Neglect to maintain connections:** Building

The Importance of Networking in Business and Personal Life

Networking is one of the most powerful tools for achieving success in both business and personal life. At its core, networking is about creating meaningful relationships that lead to mutual growth, knowledge sharing, and opportunities. Whether you're an entrepreneur, a corporate professional, or someone focused on personal growth, the value of networking cannot be overstated. In this section, we'll explore why networking is so crucial and how it impacts both your business and personal life.

1. Networking in Business: Unlocking Opportunities

In the business world, networking plays a vital role in creating opportunities, building partnerships, and establishing a reputation. Here are the key reasons why networking is essential in business:

A. Opening Doors to New Opportunities

One of the most immediate benefits of networking in business is access to opportunities that may not be available through traditional channels. Networking connects you with people who can offer new business ventures, client referrals, job openings, or investment opportunities. Often, the best opportunities arise through word of mouth and recommendations within trusted circles.

> For example, if you're an entrepreneur looking for funding or partnerships, a strong network can introduce you to potential investors or collaborators. Similarly, if you're seeking new clients, people within your network can refer you to contacts who need your services, giving you a competitive edge.

B. Building a Strong Business Reputation

Networking allows you to showcase your expertise, skills, and professionalism. By consistently engaging with others and offering value, you establish yourself as a reliable and credible figure in your industry. Over time, your network will start to view you as a thought leader or a go-to person in your field.

A strong reputation is a key factor in business success. When people trust and respect you, they are more likely to recommend your services, collaborate with you, or seek your advice. The more visible you are within your professional network, the more opportunities you'll have to build a reputation that supports your business goals.

C. Learning from Others

Networking offers a valuable opportunity to learn from the experiences and insights of others. When you engage with a diverse range of professionals, you gain access to different perspectives, innovative ideas, and strategies that can help you improve your business. Learning from others' successes and failures can also help you avoid common pitfalls and make more informed decisions.

Attending industry events, joining professional associations, or participating in online business communities allows you to stay informed about the latest trends, technologies, and best practices. This continuous learning keeps your business competitive and adaptable in a fast-paced market.

D. Forming Strategic Partnerships

Business is often built on partnerships, and networking is a key driver of forming these relationships. By connecting with people who share similar goals or complementary skills, you can develop partnerships that help both parties grow. Whether it's a joint venture, a co-marketing campaign, or a strategic collaboration, partnerships formed through networking can lead to significant business growth.

Networking also fosters relationships with mentors, advisors, and industry experts who can offer guidance and support as you navigate business challenges. Having these relationships can accelerate your growth by providing access to resources, knowledge, and connections that would otherwise be difficult to obtain.

2. Networking in Personal Life: Expanding Your Horizons

While networking is often associated with business, its benefits extend to personal life as well. Here's how networking impacts your personal development and overall well-being:

A. Personal Growth and Self-Improvement

Networking provides a platform for personal growth and self-improvement. By interacting with a wide range of people, you gain exposure to new ideas, cultures, and perspectives that can challenge your thinking and broaden your worldview. These interactions foster intellectual curiosity, helping you develop as an individual.

Moreover, networking allows you to learn from people who have skills, knowledge, or experiences that you aspire to have. By surrounding yourself with successful, motivated individuals, you're more likely to adopt their positive habits, attitudes, and approaches to life, leading to personal growth.

B. Building a Support System

In both personal and professional life, having a strong support system is invaluable. Networking helps you build relationships with people who can offer advice, encouragement, and assistance when you need it most. Whether it's finding a job, dealing with a personal challenge, or seeking guidance in a new venture, your network can provide the support you need to navigate life's ups and downs.

Your personal network might include family, friends, mentors, colleagues, or acquaintances who can offer emotional, intellectual, and sometimes even financial support. Knowing that you have people you can rely on increases your confidence and resilience in the face of challenges.

C. Increasing Your Confidence

Effective networking can significantly boost your self-confidence. Engaging with others, sharing your ideas, and learning from successful individuals can help you overcome self-doubt and develop a stronger sense of self-worth. The positive reinforcement you receive from a supportive network encourages you to take risks and pursue new opportunities, both in your career and personal life.

As you grow more comfortable with networking, you'll also become more confident in your ability to connect with people, communicate your ideas, and establish valuable relationships. This increased confidence has a ripple effect on other areas of your life, from pursuing leadership roles to engaging in new experiences.

D. Enhancing Social Connections

Networking is not just about professional connections—it's about building social relationships as well. Engaging in meaningful conversations and building rapport with people outside of your immediate circle enriches your personal life. These connections can lead to friendships, shared experiences, and a sense of belonging in both your personal and professional communities.

Moreover, maintaining a diverse network of people from various industries, backgrounds, and cultures helps you develop empathy and understanding. These connections make you more socially adept, improving your ability to relate to others in different situations, whether in casual social settings or professional environments.

Tips for Building and Maintaining Valuable Relationships

Building and maintaining valuable relationships is a crucial skill that can significantly enhance your personal and professional life. Whether you're networking for business, seeking mentorship, or developing friendships, the ability to form genuine connections can lead to numerous opportunities, support systems, and mutual growth. Here are some practical tips for creating and nurturing relationships that matter.

1. Be Authentic

Authenticity is the foundation of any meaningful relationship. People can sense when someone is being insincere or putting on a façade. To build trust, be yourself and express your true thoughts and feelings. Share your experiences, passions, and vulnerabilities, and encourage others to do the same. Authenticity fosters a deeper connection, making it easier for others to relate to you and feel comfortable opening up in return.

2. Listen Actively

Listening is just as important as talking when it comes to building relationships. Active listening involves fully concentrating on what the other person is saying without planning your response while they speak. Show genuine interest in their thoughts and feelings by nodding, maintaining eye contact, and asking clarifying questions. This not only makes the other person feel valued but also helps you understand their perspective better.

3. Offer Help and Support

One of the most effective ways to build strong relationships is by being a source of support for others. Whether it's offering advice, sharing resources, or simply being there during tough times, showing that you care and are willing to help creates a sense of reciprocity. People are more likely to remember and appreciate those who have been there for them when they needed it.

4. Stay in Touch Regularly

Once you've established a connection, it's essential to maintain it. Regular check-ins, even if brief, can go a long way in nurturing relationships. Send a quick message, share an interesting article, or ask how they've been doing. Consistent communication keeps the relationship alive and shows that you value the other person's presence in your life.

5. Personalize Your Interactions

Personalizing your interactions helps you stand out and demonstrates that you care. Reference specific conversations you've had in the past or inquire about important events in their life. Remembering details, such as birthdays or significant achievements, adds a personal touch that strengthens your connection.

6. Be Reliable and Trustworthy

Trust is a cornerstone of valuable relationships. To build trust, be reliable and consistent in your actions. Follow through on commitments, respect confidentiality, and be honest in your dealings. When others know they can count on you, it fosters a sense of security that encourages deeper connections.

7. Engage in Shared Activities

Participating in activities that interest both parties can help strengthen your bond. Whether it's joining a sports league, attending workshops, or simply going out for coffee, shared experiences create lasting memories and deepen relationships. These activities provide opportunities for meaningful conversations and interactions outside the usual setting.

8. Show Gratitude

Expressing gratitude is a powerful way to enhance relationships. A simple thank-you note, an appreciative email, or even a verbal acknowledgment can leave a lasting impression. Recognizing the efforts and contributions of others not only makes them feel valued but also encourages a positive atmosphere in your interactions.

9. Embrace Diversity

Building relationships with people from diverse backgrounds and experiences enriches your life. Embrace differences in perspective, culture, and ideas. Engaging with diverse individuals broadens your horizons, enhances your understanding of the world, and fosters creativity. It also allows you to build a more extensive network, which can lead to new opportunities.

10. Be Patient

Building valuable relationships takes time. Don't rush the process or expect immediate results. Allow the relationship to develop organically, and be patient as trust and familiarity grow.

Nurture the connection consistently, and don't be discouraged if things don't progress as quickly as you'd like.

11. Know When to Let Go

While it's essential to invest in relationships, it's also important to recognize when a connection isn't serving you or the other person. Not all relationships are meant to last, and sometimes it's necessary to let go. If a relationship feels one-sided, toxic, or draining, it may be time to reassess its value in your life.

Chapter 6: Continuous Learning and Adaptability

In an era characterized by rapid technological advancements, shifting market dynamics, and ever-evolving consumer expectations, the ability to learn continuously and adapt is no longer optional; it's essential. This chapter delves into the importance of continuous learning and adaptability, offering insights into how individuals and organizations can cultivate these qualities to thrive in a complex and competitive landscape.

The Importance of Continuous Learning

Continuous learning refers to the ongoing process of acquiring new knowledge and skills throughout one's life. It involves formal education, self-directed learning, experiential learning, and professional development. Here are several reasons why continuous learning is vital:

1. Staying Relevant in a Changing World

The business landscape is constantly changing due to technological innovations and changing consumer preferences. Continuous learning enables individuals to stay current with industry trends and advancements, ensuring they remain relevant in their fields. Professionals who commit to lifelong learning are better equipped to respond to changes and leverage new opportunities, making them invaluable assets to their organizations.

2. Enhancing Problem-Solving Skills

A commitment to continuous learning fosters critical thinking and problem-solving skills. By exposing yourself to diverse perspectives and new ideas, you develop the ability to analyze complex situations, consider various solutions, and make informed decisions. This skill set is essential for navigating challenges in both personal and professional contexts.

3. Fostering Innovation

Organizations that prioritize continuous learning create a culture of innovation. When employees are encouraged to learn and experiment, they feel empowered to explore new ideas and take calculated risks. This innovation culture can lead to the development of new products, services, or processes that enhance efficiency and improve customer satisfaction.

4. Boosting Confidence and Resilience

Continuous learning builds confidence. As you acquire new skills and knowledge, you become more self-assured in your abilities. This confidence translates into resilience, enabling you to face challenges with a positive mindset. A learner's attitude helps you bounce back from setbacks and embrace change rather than fear it.

5. Creating Networking Opportunities

Engaging in continuous learning often involves connecting with others who share similar interests. Whether through workshops, seminars, or online courses, you have the opportunity to expand your professional network. These connections can lead to collaboration, mentorship, and valuable partnerships that enhance your career.

Strategies for Continuous Learning

To cultivate a mindset of continuous learning, individuals can adopt various strategies. Here are some effective approaches:

1. Set Learning Goals

Establish clear learning goals that align with your career aspirations and interests. Goals should be specific, measurable, achievable, relevant, and time-bound (SMART). Setting clear objectives helps you stay focused and motivated while providing a framework for tracking your progress.

2. Embrace Lifelong Learning Mindset

Adopt a mindset that values curiosity and a desire for knowledge. Approach learning as an ongoing journey rather than a destination. Cultivating a lifelong learning mindset means recognizing that every experience, whether formal or informal, presents an opportunity to learn.

3. Leverage Online Resources

The digital age has made learning more accessible than ever. Utilize online platforms, such as Coursera, edX, LinkedIn Learning, and YouTube, to access courses, tutorials, and webinars on various topics. These resources allow you to learn at your own pace and tailor your education to your specific needs.

4. Participate in Workshops and Conferences

Attending workshops, conferences, and industry events provides opportunities to learn from experts, gain insights into emerging trends, and connect with peers. Engage in discussions, ask questions, and take notes to maximize your learning experience during these events.

5. Join Professional Associations

Professional associations often offer resources for continuous learning, including training programs, certifications, and networking opportunities. Joining these organizations allows you to stay informed about industry developments and access educational materials that enhance your expertise.

6. Seek Feedback and Mentorship

Feedback is a powerful tool for growth. Actively seek constructive criticism from peers, supervisors, or mentors. This feedback can provide valuable insights into areas for improvement and guide your learning efforts. Additionally, finding a mentor can help you navigate your learning journey by providing guidance, support, and accountability.

7. Engage in Self-Directed Learning

Take charge of your learning by identifying topics or skills you want to explore. Read books, listen to podcasts, and watch educational videos on subjects that interest you. Self-directed learning empowers you to take ownership of your education and pursue knowledge at your own pace.

The Importance of Adaptability

Adaptability is the ability to adjust to new conditions and respond effectively to changes in the environment. In a world marked by uncertainty, adaptability is a crucial trait that enables individuals and organizations to thrive. Here are several reasons why adaptability is essential:

1. Navigating Change

Change is inevitable, whether in personal life or within an organization. Those who can adapt quickly to new circumstances are better positioned to navigate challenges and seize opportunities. Adaptability allows you to embrace change rather than resist it, turning potential obstacles into stepping stones for success.

2. Enhancing Problem-Solving Abilities

Adaptability enhances your problem-solving capabilities. When faced with unexpected challenges, adaptable individuals can think creatively and explore alternative solutions. This flexibility enables you to approach problems with a positive mindset and find innovative ways to overcome obstacles.

3. Fostering Resilience

Resilience and adaptability go hand in hand. Being adaptable allows you to bounce back from setbacks and learn from failures. Instead of being discouraged by difficulties, adaptable individuals view challenges as opportunities for growth and development, leading to greater resilience in the face of adversity.

4. Promoting Collaboration and Teamwork

Adaptable individuals are often more effective collaborators. They can work well with diverse teams, accommodating different perspectives and adapting their approaches to achieve common goals. This flexibility fosters a positive team dynamic, enhancing communication and collaboration among team members.

5. Staying Competitive

In a competitive job market, adaptability is a key differentiator. Employers value individuals who can thrive in changing environments, learn new skills quickly, and take on different roles as needed. Being adaptable not only enhances your employability but also positions you as a valuable asset within your organization.

Strategies for Cultivating Adaptability

To develop adaptability, individuals can implement several strategies:

1. Embrace a Growth Mindset

Adopting a growth mindset is essential for adaptability. This mindset fosters the belief that abilities and intelligence can be developed through dedication and hard work. Embrace challenges as opportunities to learn and grow, and view failures as stepping stones to success.

2. Stay Informed

Stay abreast of industry trends, market changes, and emerging technologies that may impact your field. This awareness allows you to anticipate changes and prepare accordingly. Engage with industry news, join relevant forums, and follow thought leaders to stay informed about developments.

3. Practice Flexibility

Cultivate a flexible approach to your work and personal life. Be open to change and willing to adjust your plans as needed. Practicing flexibility can involve taking on new responsibilities, exploring different roles within your organization, or being open to new ideas and perspectives.

4. Develop Problem-Solving Skills

Strengthen your problem-solving abilities by seeking opportunities to tackle challenges. When faced with a problem, take time to analyze the situation, brainstorm potential solutions, and assess their effectiveness. The more you practice problem-solving, the more adaptable you'll become in navigating complex situations.

5. Reflect on Experiences

Take time to reflect on your experiences, both positive and negative. Consider what you learned from each situation and how you adapted. Reflection helps you identify patterns in your behavior and decision-making, allowing you to become more self-aware and better prepared for future challenges.

6. Seek Diverse Experiences

Engage in activities outside your comfort zone to build adaptability. Volunteer for projects that require new skills, attend workshops on unfamiliar topics, or travel to new places. Exposing yourself to different experiences enhances your ability to adjust to new situations and perspectives.

7. Maintain a Support Network

Surround yourself with a supportive network of colleagues, friends, and mentors. These connections provide encouragement during challenging times and can offer valuable insights when navigating change. Lean on your support network to gain perspective and seek advice when faced with uncertainty.

Lifelong Learning as a Key to Success

In a fast-paced, ever-changing world, the concept of lifelong learning has evolved from a choice to a necessity for personal and professional success. Lifelong learning refers to the continuous pursuit of knowledge and skills, regardless of age or career stage. It goes beyond formal education and encompasses self-directed learning, experiential learning, and opportunities for personal growth. This sub-chapter explores the importance of lifelong learning and its role as a crucial driver of success.

1. Staying Competitive in a Changing World

One of the most compelling reasons to embrace lifelong learning is the need to stay competitive in today's rapidly evolving landscape. Technology is advancing at breakneck speed, and industries are constantly transforming. Jobs that were in demand a few years ago may become obsolete tomorrow. To stay relevant and competitive, individuals must continuously update their skills and knowledge.

By engaging in lifelong learning, you can adapt to these changes and position yourself as a valuable asset to employers or clients. It ensures that you are up-to-date with industry trends, emerging technologies, and best practices, giving you a competitive edge in your field. Moreover, being proactive about learning can open doors to new opportunities, career growth, and even leadership roles.

2. Enhancing Problem-Solving and Critical Thinking

Lifelong learning helps sharpen your critical thinking and problem-solving abilities. As you expose yourself to new information, diverse perspectives, and different ways of thinking, you develop the skills needed to analyze complex situations and find innovative solutions. In both personal and professional settings, the ability to solve problems efficiently and creatively is highly valued.

Learning new skills or exploring unfamiliar subjects challenges your mind and pushes you out of your comfort zone. This mental exercise improves cognitive function, making you more adaptable and better equipped to tackle obstacles that arise. Whether it's mastering a new software, learning a foreign language, or delving into a completely different field, lifelong learning fosters intellectual growth that enhances your overall ability to think critically.

3. Fostering Personal Growth and Fulfillment

Lifelong learning is not just about career success—it also contributes significantly to personal growth and fulfillment. The act of learning ignites curiosity and encourages you to explore new interests, develop hobbies, and discover new passions. It adds richness to your life by expanding your knowledge beyond the confines of your professional work.

Engaging in continuous learning also boosts your self-confidence. As you acquire new skills and achieve personal milestones, you feel a sense of accomplishment and empowerment. This confidence can carry over into other areas of life, encouraging you to set new goals and pursue ambitions you might have previously thought unattainable.

Moreover, lifelong learning often leads to a deeper understanding of the world around you. Whether you're learning about history, culture, or human psychology, the knowledge you gain enhances your ability to empathize with others, appreciate diversity, and approach life with a more open mind.

4. Increasing Adaptability and Resilience

In a world where change is the only constant, the ability to adapt is essential for long-term success. Lifelong learners are more adaptable because they are accustomed to acquiring new skills, processing new information, and evolving with changing circumstances. This adaptability makes them better equipped to handle unexpected challenges, career transitions, or shifts in industry demands.

Resilience, too, is a byproduct of lifelong learning. The process of learning often involves facing new challenges, making mistakes, and overcoming obstacles. By continuously pushing yourself to grow and develop, you build resilience and learn to approach difficulties with a positive, growth-oriented mindset.

For example, if you encounter a roadblock in your career—whether it's a layoff, industry disruption, or a personal setback—having a foundation of continuous learning will give you the tools to pivot, re-skill, and move forward with confidence.

5. Building a Broader Network

Lifelong learning can also expand your professional and social networks. Whether you're attending workshops, enrolling in online courses, or joining industry groups, you're bound to meet like-minded individuals who share your interests and goals. These connections can lead to valuable partnerships, collaborations, and mentorship opportunities.

Networking is not only about forming professional relationships—it also creates opportunities for personal growth. Engaging with others who are equally committed to lifelong learning exposes you to diverse viewpoints, fosters meaningful conversations, and creates a sense of community. The broader your network, the more opportunities you'll have for learning and growth, both personally and professionally.

Staying Adaptable in a Rapidly Changing Environment

In today's fast-paced world, the only constant is change. Technological advancements, shifting market dynamics, and evolving consumer expectations are just a few factors that can disrupt established norms and practices. As a result, adaptability has emerged as a crucial skill for individuals and organizations alike. Staying adaptable means being open to change, willing to learn new skills, and able to pivot when circumstances dictate. Here are some strategies to help you remain adaptable in a rapidly changing environment.

1. Embrace a Growth Mindset

A growth mindset is the belief that abilities and intelligence can be developed through dedication and hard work. This mindset encourages individuals to view challenges as opportunities for growth rather than obstacles. When faced with change, those with a growth mindset are more likely to embrace new learning experiences, seek solutions, and persist in the face of adversity.

To cultivate a growth mindset, actively challenge your assumptions and be willing to learn from failures. Reflect on past experiences and consider what lessons you can apply to future challenges. By focusing on continuous improvement, you'll develop the resilience needed to adapt to any situation.

2. Stay Informed

In a rapidly changing environment, staying informed about industry trends, technological advancements, and emerging best practices is essential. Knowledge is power; the more you understand the context in which you operate, the better equipped you will be to respond to changes.

To keep yourself informed, regularly read industry publications, follow thought leaders on social media, and participate in webinars or workshops. Engaging with professional networks and communities can also provide valuable insights and keep you abreast of developments in your field.

3. Develop Problem-Solving Skills

Adaptability is closely tied to effective problem-solving. When faced with unexpected challenges, the ability to think critically and devise creative solutions is invaluable. To enhance your problem-solving skills, practice approaching problems methodically: define the issue, gather relevant information, brainstorm potential solutions, and evaluate the best course of action.

Engaging in activities that require strategic thinking, such as puzzles, games, or team-based projects, can also help sharpen your problem-solving abilities. The more you practice, the more confident you will become in navigating uncertainty.

4. Cultivate Emotional Intelligence

Emotional intelligence (EI) refers to the ability to recognize, understand, and manage your emotions and the emotions of others. High EI enables you to navigate change more effectively by fostering better communication, collaboration, and conflict resolution.

To develop your emotional intelligence, practice self-awareness by reflecting on your emotional responses to various situations. Pay attention to how your feelings influence your decisions and interactions. Additionally, work on empathy by actively listening to others and trying to understand their perspectives. By enhancing your emotional intelligence, you'll be better equipped to adapt to changing circumstances while maintaining positive relationships.

5. Be Open to Feedback

Feedback is a valuable tool for personal and professional growth. Being open to constructive criticism can help you identify areas for improvement and adjust your approach accordingly. Create an environment where feedback is welcomed, whether through formal evaluations or informal discussions.

Actively seek feedback from colleagues, mentors, or supervisors. Ask specific questions to gain insights into your performance and areas for development. By incorporating feedback into your learning process, you'll become more adaptable and responsive to the needs of your environment.

6. Foster a Culture of Collaboration

In a rapidly changing environment, collaboration can lead to more innovative solutions and quicker adaptation. By working with others, you can leverage diverse perspectives and experiences, enabling you to tackle challenges more effectively.

Encourage open communication and knowledge-sharing among team members. Create opportunities for collaboration through team projects, brainstorming sessions, or workshops. By fostering a collaborative culture, you'll not only enhance adaptability but also build stronger relationships within your organization.

7. Prioritize Continuous Learning

A commitment to lifelong learning is essential for staying adaptable. The more skills and knowledge you acquire, the better prepared you will be to handle change. Embrace opportunities for professional development, whether through formal education, online courses, or self-directed study.

Identify areas where you can improve or expand your skill set, and set specific learning goals. Allocate time for personal development each week to ensure you stay current and adaptable in your field. By prioritizing continuous learning, you'll position yourself to thrive in a dynamic environment.

8. Practice Flexibility

Flexibility is a core component of adaptability. The ability to pivot your approach in response to new information or changing circumstances is essential for success. To practice flexibility, start by being open to new ideas and perspectives, even if they challenge your established beliefs.

Engage in scenarios that require you to adjust your plans or approaches. For example, when working on a project, be willing to revise your strategy based on feedback or new developments.

By training yourself to be more flexible, you'll find it easier to adapt to unforeseen challenges.

Chapter 7: Time Management and Productivity

Time is one of the most precious resources in the business world, and mastering the art of managing it effectively is crucial for success. In business, it's not just about working hard, but working smart. Entrepreneurs and business professionals who can harness the power of time management often find themselves more productive, focused, and able to achieve their goals. In this chapter, we will explore practical time management techniques and strategies for boosting productivity.

1. The Importance of Time Management

Time is the only resource that is equally distributed to everyone. Whether you're a student, an entrepreneur, or a seasoned business executive, you have 24 hours in a day. How you use these hours can determine your level of success. Proper time management allows you to:

- Focus on important tasks.
- Reduce stress and prevent burnout.
- Improve decision-making.
- Maximize productivity.

Time management isn't just about cramming more tasks into your day, but about organizing your time in a way that aligns with your priorities and goals.

2. Setting SMART Goals

Effective time management starts with goal setting. If you don't know what you're trying to achieve, you won't know how to manage your time to achieve it. The SMART goal framework—Specific, Measurable, Achievable, Relevant, and Time-bound—helps you create clear and actionable objectives.

- **Specific**: Define exactly what you want to achieve. Vague goals like "be successful" aren't actionable. Instead, something specific like "increase sales by 10% this quarter" gives you direction.
- **Measurable**: Your goals should be measurable so you can track your progress. If you can't measure it, you can't manage it.
- **Achievable**: Set realistic goals that are challenging but possible to reach. Ambition is good, but setting unattainable goals only leads to frustration.
- **Relevant**: Ensure that your goals align with your broader business objectives. Time management works best when your daily tasks contribute to the bigger picture.
- **Time-bound**: Every goal should have a deadline. Deadlines create urgency and help you prioritize tasks.

3. Prioritization: The 80/20 Rule

One of the most effective time management principles is the 80/20 rule, also known as the Pareto Principle. It suggests that 80% of your results come from 20% of your efforts. In business, this means identifying and focusing on the tasks that have the most significant impact.

To apply this:

1. Identify your most important tasks (MITs). These are the tasks that contribute the most to your goals.
2. Focus on these tasks during your peak productivity hours.
3. Delegate or minimize tasks that don't contribute as much to your overall success.

By narrowing your focus, you can maximize your productivity without spreading yourself too thin.

4. The Power of Time Blocking

Time blocking is a technique where you divide your day into blocks of time, each dedicated to specific tasks. It forces you to focus on one task at a time, reducing multitasking and distractions. Time blocking helps you:

- Set clear expectations for what needs to be done.
- Create a sense of urgency and accountability.
- Avoid procrastination by scheduling even the smallest tasks.

For instance, block time for important tasks like strategic planning, client meetings, or product development. Schedule shorter blocks for emails, administrative work, and breaks.

When time blocking, be realistic about how long each task will take. Overestimating how much you can accomplish in a given time can lead to stress, while underestimating can result in wasted time.

5. The Two-Minute Rule

Productivity often gets derailed by small, seemingly insignificant tasks. The two-minute rule helps prevent these tasks from piling up. The rule is simple: if a task will take two minutes or less, do it immediately. This applies to:

- Responding to quick emails.
- Scheduling meetings.
- Sending a quick update to a client.

By taking care of these micro-tasks right away, you avoid having them clutter your to-do list and become overwhelming later.

6. Avoiding Multitasking

Multitasking may seem like a productivity booster, but it often leads to decreased efficiency. When you switch between tasks, your brain has to reset and refocus, which takes time. Studies show that multitasking can reduce productivity by up to 40%.

Instead of multitasking:

- Focus on one task at a time.
- Use techniques like the Pomodoro Technique (25 minutes of focused work followed by a 5-minute break) to stay on track.
- Prioritize your tasks and work on them sequentially rather than trying to juggle multiple projects at once.

7. Delegation: Leveraging Your Team

As an entrepreneur or business professional, it can be tempting to do everything yourself. However, learning to delegate is essential for both time management and productivity. Delegation allows you to focus on high-priority tasks while others handle the rest.

To delegate effectively:

1. Identify tasks that don't require your direct involvement, such as administrative work or routine customer inquiries.
2. Assign tasks to team members who are skilled and capable of handling them.
3. Provide clear instructions and deadlines.

Remember, delegation is not about dumping tasks on others but empowering your team to take ownership and contribute to the business's success.

8. Overcoming Procrastination

Procrastination is the enemy of productivity. It often happens when a task feels overwhelming, boring, or difficult. However, there are ways to combat procrastination:

- **Break tasks into smaller steps**: Large projects can be intimidating, but breaking them into smaller, manageable tasks makes them less daunting.
- **Use the 5-minute rule**: Commit to working on a task for just five minutes. Often, the hardest part is starting, and once you've begun, you're more likely to continue.
- **Eliminate distractions**: Identify what tends to pull you away from your work—whether it's social media, noise, or interruptions—and take steps to eliminate these distractions during work hours.
- **Reward yourself**: Set small rewards for completing tasks. This could be something as simple as taking a break, grabbing a coffee, or doing something enjoyable.

9. Harnessing Technology for Time Management

In today's digital world, technology can be a double-edged sword. While it can be a major source of distraction, it can also significantly boost productivity when used correctly. Here are some tools to enhance your time management:

- **Task management apps**: Tools like Trello, Asana, and Todoist help you organize and prioritize tasks.
- **Time tracking apps**: Apps like Toggl or RescueTime track how you spend your time, helping you identify inefficiencies.
- **Calendar tools**: Google Calendar and Microsoft Outlook can be used to schedule meetings, block time for tasks, and set reminders.
- **Focus apps**: Apps like Focus@Will or Forest can help you stay focused by creating a distraction-free environment.

These tools can help streamline your workflow and ensure you're using your time effectively.

10. Balancing Work and Rest

Contrary to popular belief, being productive doesn't mean working non-stop. Rest and recovery are just as important as work. Overworking leads to burnout, which reduces both your creativity and productivity. Incorporate these habits to maintain a balance:

- **Schedule breaks**: Taking short, frequent breaks throughout the day helps you stay fresh and focused. Use techniques like the Pomodoro Technique to incorporate breaks into your workday.
- **Get enough sleep**: A well-rested mind is more creative and productive. Aim for 7-8 hours of sleep per night.
- **Exercise regularly**: Physical activity boosts your energy levels and mental clarity, allowing you to perform better at work.

Balancing work and rest is about working smarter, not harder. Prioritize your health and well-being to sustain long-term productivity.

11. Continuous Improvement: Reflect and Adjust

Time management is not a one-size-fits-all approach. It requires continuous evaluation and adjustment. At the end of each week or month, take time to reflect on:

- What worked well in terms of managing your time.
- What challenges you faced.
- How you can improve moving forward.

Adjust your strategies based on what you learn. Over time, you'll develop a time management system that's tailored to your needs and helps you maximize productivity.

Techniques for Maximizing Productivity: Time Blocking and Prioritization

Productivity is the lifeblood of success in both personal and professional life. Being productive means getting more done in less time, with better results, while also maintaining focus and reducing stress. However, with so many distractions and competing priorities, it can be challenging to stay on track. Fortunately, there are proven techniques, such as time blocking and prioritization, that can help you maximize productivity, stay organized, and ensure that you are working on the tasks that matter most. In this section, we'll dive deep into these two techniques and explore how you can apply them to optimize your time and effort.

1. Time Blocking: Structuring Your Day for Success

What is Time Blocking? Time blocking is a simple yet powerful technique where you divide your day into specific blocks of time, with each block dedicated to a particular task or group of tasks. Instead of working through a random to-do list or juggling multiple tasks at once, time blocking forces you to focus on one task at a time, ensuring that you give it your full attention.

For example, you might block 9 AM to 11 AM for focused, deep work (like writing a report or strategizing for a project) and 2 PM to 3 PM for responding to emails. By allocating time blocks for each activity, you can minimize distractions and make sure you're progressing on the most important tasks.

Benefits of Time Blocking:

- **Increased Focus**: By dedicating time to one task, you're less likely to get distracted or interrupted. This singular focus allows for more efficient work.
- **Better Time Management**: Time blocking helps you visualize your day and ensures that you're giving sufficient time to each activity without letting one task dominate.
- **Reduced Procrastination**: When you've assigned a specific time for a task, you're more likely to get started rather than putting it off.
- **Improved Work-Life Balance**: By blocking time for both work tasks and personal activities (like exercise, family time, or hobbies), you can create a more balanced schedule that accommodates both professional and personal priorities.

How to Implement Time Blocking:

1. **List Your Tasks**: Start by writing down everything you need to accomplish. This can include work-related tasks, personal commitments, and even breaks.
2. **Estimate the Time Required**: Next, estimate how long each task will take. Be realistic—underestimating the time required can lead to frustration and stress later on.
3. **Assign Time Blocks**: Based on the time needed for each task, allocate specific blocks in your schedule. Ensure that you're blocking time for high-priority work during your most productive hours. For example, if you're most focused in the morning, block those hours for tasks that require deep concentration.
4. **Account for Flexibility**: It's important to leave some buffer time between blocks for unexpected tasks or breaks. Life is unpredictable, and flexibility in your schedule will help you avoid feeling overwhelmed.

5. **Use Technology to Help**: Tools like Google Calendar, Microsoft Outlook, or time-blocking apps like Todoist or Clockwise can help you manage your blocks and send reminders when it's time to switch tasks.
6. **Review and Adjust**: At the end of the day or week, review your progress and see if your time blocks were realistic. Adjust them based on how the week went, and improve your scheduling for future tasks.

2. Prioritization: Working on What Truly Matters

What is Prioritization? Prioritization is the process of determining which tasks are the most important and focusing your energy on them first. With so many tasks competing for your attention, it's easy to become overwhelmed and work on what feels urgent rather than what is truly important. Prioritization helps you avoid this trap by focusing on tasks that drive the most significant results.

Prioritization helps you answer questions like:

- What tasks are critical for achieving my goals?
- What can be delegated or postponed?
- What tasks will have the most significant impact if completed first?

The Importance of Prioritization for Productivity:

- **Increases Efficiency**: By identifying and working on high-impact tasks, you can get more done in less time, focusing on what truly matters rather than wasting energy on low-priority work.
- **Reduces Overwhelm**: When everything seems important, it's easy to feel overwhelmed. Prioritization gives you clarity on what to tackle first, reducing stress and increasing confidence in your workflow.

- **Improves Decision-Making**: When you have clear priorities, it's easier to say no to distractions, unnecessary meetings, or tasks that don't align with your goals.

Techniques for Effective Prioritization:

a. The Eisenhower Matrix

One of the most effective prioritization tools is the Eisenhower Matrix, also known as the Urgent-Important Matrix. This matrix helps you sort tasks into four categories:

- **Urgent and Important**: Tasks that need immediate attention and contribute to your long-term goals. These should be tackled first.
- **Important but Not Urgent**: Tasks that are important but can be scheduled for later. These are often related to long-term planning or personal development and should be prioritized once urgent tasks are done.
- **Urgent but Not Important**: Tasks that demand immediate attention but don't significantly contribute to your long-term goals. These tasks are often distractions and should be delegated or minimized.
- **Neither Urgent Nor Important**: Tasks that neither contribute to your goals nor need immediate attention. These should be eliminated or postponed indefinitely.

Using the Eisenhower Matrix helps you separate critical tasks from distractions, ensuring that you spend your time where it will have the greatest impact.

b. The ABCDE Method

The ABCDE method is a simple prioritization tool developed by productivity expert Brian Tracy. It helps you rank your tasks by priority:

- **A Tasks**: Must be done. These tasks are essential and have serious consequences if not completed.
- **B Tasks**: Should be done. These are important, but not as critical as A tasks. They may have moderate consequences if not done.
- **C Tasks**: Nice to do. These are tasks that would be nice to complete, but there are no consequences for delaying them.
- **D Tasks**: Delegate. Tasks that can and should be delegated to someone else.
- **E Tasks**: Eliminate. These are unnecessary tasks that don't contribute to your goals and can be removed from your to-do list.

Once you've classified your tasks, start with the A tasks and work your way down. Never start a B task if there are A tasks left undone.

c. The 80/20 Rule (Pareto Principle)

The Pareto Principle, or the 80/20 rule, states that 80% of your results come from 20% of your efforts. In the context of prioritization, this means identifying the few tasks that will generate the most significant outcomes and focusing your energy on those.

For example, if you run a business, 20% of your clients might account for 80% of your revenue. By prioritizing work that benefits these clients, you maximize your impact without spreading yourself too thin. Similarly, in your personal life, 20% of your habits may contribute to 80% of your well-being. Identifying and nurturing these habits will yield the greatest results.

d. MITs (Most Important Tasks)

MITs are the top 1-3 tasks that you must accomplish each day to consider your day successful. By identifying your MITs, you can ensure that even if the rest of your day gets derailed, you've completed the most critical work.

To use this method:

1. At the beginning of each day, list the top 1-3 tasks that must get done.
2. Block out time in your schedule (preferably during your peak productivity hours) to focus solely on these tasks.
3. Work on your MITs before anything else—before checking email, attending meetings, or handling less important tasks.

3. Combining Time Blocking and Prioritization for Maximum Productivity

Time blocking and prioritization are two techniques that work well together to create a structured and focused workday. Here's how to combine them effectively:

- **Prioritize First**: Before you start time blocking, prioritize your tasks for the day or week. Use techniques like the Eisenhower Matrix or MITs to identify which tasks are the most important and deserve the majority of your focus.
- **Time Block Your Priorities**: Once you've identified your priorities, assign specific time blocks in your schedule for each task. Make sure you're dedicating time to your most important and high-impact tasks, particularly during your most productive hours.
- **Use Buffer Time for Low-Priority Tasks**: After blocking time for your top priorities, use any remaining time to handle lower-priority tasks, administrative work, or breaks.

By combining these two techniques, you can ensure that you're not only working efficiently but also focusing on the right tasks at the right times.

The Importance of Work-Life Balance

In today's fast-paced, highly connected world, the boundary between work and personal life often becomes blurred. Many professionals, particularly entrepreneurs and business leaders, find themselves consumed by their work, which can lead to burnout, stress, and even long-term health problems. Achieving a healthy work-life balance is essential not just for personal well-being, but also for sustained professional success.

1. Defining Work-Life Balance

Work-life balance refers to the equilibrium between the demands of work and the personal time needed for relaxation, family, hobbies, and self-care. It involves striking a balance where neither work nor personal life dominates, allowing both aspects to coexist in harmony. While the concept may seem simple, in practice, achieving this balance can be challenging, especially in high-pressure environments or fast-paced industries.

It's important to recognize that work-life balance isn't about rigidly splitting time between work and personal life. Instead, it's about being flexible and adjusting based on changing priorities. Some periods of life may require more focus on work, while others may necessitate more personal time. The key is to maintain an overall sense of harmony rather than a strict 50-50 division.

2. Why Work-Life Balance is Critical

Maintaining a proper work-life balance is critical for several reasons:

- **Mental and Physical Health**: Overworking leads to chronic stress, which can cause serious health issues such as anxiety, depression, and heart disease. On the other hand, adequate rest, relaxation, and personal fulfillment improve overall well-being. A balanced life allows the mind and body to recharge, leading to improved health and a lower risk of burnout.
- **Increased Productivity**: It may seem counterintuitive, but working long hours doesn't always equate to higher productivity. Studies have shown that people who maintain a healthy work-life balance tend to be more focused and efficient during work hours. A well-rested mind is sharper, more creative, and more capable of handling complex tasks.
- **Job Satisfaction**: People who strike a balance between their work and personal life are often more satisfied with their jobs. They feel a sense of control and fulfillment, which makes work more enjoyable and less stressful. Conversely, those who feel trapped by work obligations can quickly grow resentful, decreasing motivation and enthusiasm.
- **Better Relationships**: When work takes over, relationships often suffer. Whether it's with family, friends, or a partner, neglecting personal relationships in favor of work can strain connections and lead to isolation. Maintaining a balance allows time for nurturing these important relationships, which in turn creates a supportive network that enhances both personal and professional life.
- **Sustainable Success**: True success isn't just about achieving career goals—it's about maintaining that success over the long term. Without a proper balance, the drive for career success can lead to burnout, which can derail professional progress. A balanced approach ensures that you have the energy and mental clarity to sustain your achievements over time.

3. Consequences of Poor Work-Life Balance

Failing to achieve a healthy balance between work and personal life can have far-reaching consequences, not just for individuals but also for businesses and teams. Some of the potential risks include:

- **Burnout**: Burnout is one of the most common results of poor work-life balance. This state of emotional, mental, and physical exhaustion is often caused by prolonged stress, and it can have devastating effects on a person's career, health, and personal life. Symptoms of burnout include fatigue, lack of motivation, irritability, and a sense of detachment from work.
- **Decreased Productivity**: When people are overworked and stressed, their productivity often decreases. Tasks take longer to complete, decision-making becomes clouded, and creativity is stifled. The quality of work may also suffer, leading to mistakes and inefficiencies.
- **Health Problems**: Chronic stress caused by poor work-life balance can lead to various health issues, including insomnia, high blood pressure, heart disease, and a weakened immune system. Mental health can also deteriorate, with increased risks of anxiety and depression.
- **Strained Relationships**: Overworking can lead to neglecting personal relationships, which may create emotional distance or conflict with loved ones. This strain can cause feelings of loneliness and further increase stress, creating a negative cycle.
- **Poor Employee Retention**: In the business world, companies that do not prioritize work-life balance often experience higher turnover rates. Employees who feel overburdened are more likely to seek new job opportunities that offer a more balanced lifestyle.

4. Strategies for Achieving Work-Life Balance

Work-life balance may seem elusive, but it can be achieved with conscious effort and strategic planning. Here are some effective strategies to help maintain this balance:

a. Set Boundaries

One of the most important steps in achieving work-life balance is setting clear boundaries between work and personal time. This means defining specific hours for work and ensuring that personal time is respected. Boundaries also involve saying no to excessive work demands that infringe upon personal commitments.

- **Create a Daily Schedule**: Plan your day to include time for both work and personal activities. Stick to this schedule as much as possible to avoid letting work spill into personal time.
- **Communicate Your Boundaries**: Let your colleagues, team members, and supervisors know your work hours and when you are unavailable. This sets clear expectations and reduces the pressure to be constantly accessible.

b. Prioritize Self-Care

Self-care isn't a luxury—it's a necessity for maintaining balance. Prioritizing your health and well-being should always be at the top of your list.

- **Get Regular Exercise**: Physical activity helps reduce stress, boost energy levels, and improve mental clarity. Whether it's going for a run, doing yoga, or even a brisk walk, make time for movement.
- **Sleep Well**: Sleep is essential for mental and physical recovery. Aim for 7-8 hours of quality sleep each night to recharge and stay productive during the day.

- **Practice Mindfulness**: Incorporating mindfulness practices such as meditation, deep breathing, or journaling can help reduce stress and improve focus. These techniques allow you to be more present in both your work and personal life.

c. Delegate and Outsource

Trying to do everything yourself is a recipe for burnout. Whether at work or in your personal life, it's important to delegate tasks to others when possible. In a business setting, this may involve assigning responsibilities to team members. In your personal life, it could mean outsourcing chores like cleaning, grocery shopping, or other time-consuming tasks.

d. Take Breaks

Regular breaks are crucial for maintaining focus and avoiding burnout. Incorporating short breaks throughout your workday helps you stay energized and prevents fatigue.

- **The Pomodoro Technique**: This method involves working for 25 minutes and then taking a 5-minute break. After four cycles, take a longer 15-30 minute break. This structured break schedule helps maintain high levels of productivity while giving your brain time to rest.
- **Vacation Time**: Don't underestimate the power of taking a vacation. Time away from work allows you to fully recharge and come back with renewed energy and creativity.

e. Unplug from Technology

While technology has made it easier to stay connected, it can also blur the lines between work and personal life. Constantly checking emails or being available 24/7 can lead to exhaustion and burnout.

- **Set Limits on Technology Use**: Establish rules around when and how often you will check emails or take work calls. For example, avoid checking your phone after a certain hour in the evening or during weekends.
- **Designate Tech-Free Zones**: Create specific areas in your home where technology is off-limits, such as the dining table or bedroom. This encourages more meaningful, tech-free interactions with family and friends.

5. Workplace Policies That Support Work-Life Balance

Businesses can play a significant role in helping employees achieve work-life balance. In fact, companies that promote a balanced lifestyle often see higher levels of productivity, employee satisfaction, and retention. Here are some policies that can support work-life balance in the workplace:

- **Flexible Work Hours**: Offering flexible schedules allows employees to manage their personal and professional lives more effectively. This can include options like remote work, compressed workweeks, or staggered hours.
- **Encouraging Time Off**: Businesses should encourage employees to use their vacation time and take regular breaks. Encouraging time away from work helps prevent burnout and fosters a healthier, more productive workforce.
- **Wellness Programs**: Implementing wellness initiatives such as fitness programs, mental health support, and stress management workshops can help employees maintain a healthy work-life balance.

Chapter 8: Cultivating a Positive Mindset

In the journey toward personal and professional success, one of the most critical but often overlooked elements is mindset. Your mindset shapes how you see the world, how you approach challenges, and how resilient you are in the face of adversity. A positive mindset not only improves your emotional and mental well-being, but it also enhances your ability to perform, make decisions, and interact with others.

Cultivating a positive mindset isn't just about feeling good; it's about shifting your perspective to see opportunities where others see obstacles, to learn from failure, and to maintain motivation even when the going gets tough. This chapter will explore why mindset is so important, the characteristics of a positive mindset, and practical strategies you can use to develop and strengthen it.

1. What is a Positive Mindset?

A positive mindset is an optimistic mental attitude that focuses on the good in situations, emphasizes possibilities, and seeks solutions rather than dwelling on problems. It doesn't mean ignoring negative aspects or pretending everything is perfect, but rather approaching life with a proactive and constructive outlook. People with positive mindsets are generally more resilient, motivated, and able to navigate life's challenges with greater ease.

There are two major types of mindsets that impact success: fixed mindset and growth mindset. A **fixed mindset** assumes that abilities and intelligence are static and cannot be changed. In contrast, a **growth mindset**, as defined by psychologist Carol Dweck, is the belief that abilities and intelligence can be developed through dedication and hard work. A positive mindset is deeply rooted in this idea of growth.

Key Traits of a Positive Mindset:

- **Optimism**: Viewing challenges as opportunities to learn and grow rather than as roadblocks.
- **Resilience**: The ability to recover quickly from setbacks and failures.
- **Gratitude**: Focusing on what's going well in life, rather than on what's lacking.
- **Self-Belief**: Trusting in your abilities to overcome challenges and achieve goals.
- **Solution-Oriented Thinking**: Looking for solutions rather than fixating on problems.
- **Adaptability**: Being open to change and flexible in your approach to obstacles.

2. The Importance of a Positive Mindset

A positive mindset influences nearly every aspect of life, from relationships and career success to mental and physical health. Here's why cultivating a positive mindset is essential:

a. Improved Mental Health

A positive mindset fosters emotional resilience, helping you to cope with stress, anxiety, and depression more effectively. When you focus on solutions rather than problems, it reduces the feeling of being overwhelmed. Positive thinkers are also more likely to engage in healthy habits that support mental well-being, such as practicing mindfulness, gratitude, and self-compassion.

b. Increased Productivity and Performance

Optimism and a growth mindset lead to greater perseverance in the face of challenges, which can significantly boost productivity. When you believe that effort leads to improvement, you are more likely to push through difficulties and complete tasks, even when they seem hard. This can result in increased focus, creativity, and overall job satisfaction.

c. Better Relationships

A positive mindset can enhance your relationships by fostering more effective communication, empathy, and emotional intelligence. Positive people are often seen as more approachable, collaborative, and supportive, which can lead to stronger personal and professional relationships.

d. Greater Success and Goal Achievement

Research shows that people with a positive mindset are more likely to set and achieve ambitious goals. By focusing on potential solutions and opportunities, rather than obstacles, you open yourself up to possibilities that others may overlook. Moreover, the confidence and self-belief that come with a positive mindset make it easier to pursue new opportunities and take calculated risks that lead to success.

e. Physical Health Benefits

The mind-body connection is powerful. Numerous studies have shown that a positive mindset can contribute to better physical health. Optimism has been linked to lower levels of stress, which in turn leads to better heart health, a stronger immune system, and reduced risk of chronic diseases. People with a positive outlook are also more likely to engage in healthy behaviors, such as regular exercise, proper nutrition, and getting adequate rest.

3. How to Cultivate a Positive Mindset

While some people naturally lean toward optimism, cultivating a positive mindset is a skill that can be learned and developed over time. Here are practical strategies you can use to nurture and strengthen your positive mindset.

a. Practice Gratitude

Gratitude is one of the most powerful tools for shifting your mindset. When you focus on what you're grateful for, it becomes easier to see the positive in any situation.

- **Daily Gratitude Journal**: Start or end your day by writing down three things you are grateful for. They can be as simple as enjoying a good cup of coffee or having a supportive friend. This habit trains your brain to look for the good in your life, which over time creates a more positive outlook.
- **Gratitude Reflection**: When facing challenges, take a moment to reflect on what the situation is teaching you or how it might lead to personal growth. Even tough experiences often have silver linings if you look closely.

b. Reframe Negative Thoughts

Negative thoughts are inevitable, but how you respond to them can make all the difference. Instead of allowing them to dominate your mindset, practice reframing them into more constructive thoughts.

- **Challenge Limiting Beliefs**: When a negative thought arises, such as "I'm not good enough" or "I'll never succeed," ask yourself if it's really true. What evidence supports this belief? Often, you'll find that your negative thoughts are based on fear or insecurity rather than fact.
- **Turn Obstacles into Opportunities**: For every negative thought, find a way to reframe it into an opportunity for growth. For example, instead of thinking "This project is too difficult," try reframing it as "This project is challenging, but it's an opportunity to develop new skills."

c. Surround Yourself with Positivity

Your environment plays a significant role in shaping your mindset. The people you interact with, the media you consume, and the spaces you inhabit all influence your mental state.

- **Positive Relationships**: Surround yourself with people who uplift, support, and inspire you. Limit time spent with individuals who are consistently negative or drain your energy. Positive relationships encourage growth and reinforce a positive outlook.
- **Curate Your Media**: Pay attention to the media and content you consume. Does it inspire and educate you, or does it create fear, anxiety, or negativity? Curating a positive media diet—whether it's books, podcasts, or social media—can help reinforce a growth-oriented mindset.

d. Focus on What You Can Control

One of the biggest obstacles to a positive mindset is focusing on things that are outside of your control. This can lead to frustration, helplessness, and anxiety. Instead, focus on what you can influence.

- **Control the Controllables**: Ask yourself, "What can I control in this situation?" Focusing on actionable steps helps you regain a sense of power and keeps you moving forward.
- **Let Go of Perfectionism**: Perfectionism often leads to feelings of inadequacy and stress. Accept that mistakes and setbacks are part of the learning process. Instead of striving for perfection, aim for progress. This mindset shift reduces pressure and allows you to take risks without fear of failure.

e. Practice Self-Compassion

Being kind to yourself is a crucial element of maintaining a positive mindset. We often hold ourselves to unrealistic standards, which can lead to self-criticism and feelings of inadequacy. Self-compassion allows you to acknowledge your mistakes and shortcomings without judgment.

- **Treat Yourself Like a Friend**: When you're going through a tough time, ask yourself how you would support a friend in a similar situation. Then, offer that same kindness and encouragement to yourself.
- **Acknowledge Your Efforts**: Celebrate small wins and recognize the effort you're putting into your growth and progress. This builds confidence and reinforces a positive outlook on your abilities.

f. Set Realistic and Achievable Goals

Setting clear, realistic goals gives you a sense of direction and purpose. When you work toward meaningful objectives, it fuels motivation and positivity.

- **Break Down Big Goals**: Large, long-term goals can feel overwhelming. Break them down into smaller, more manageable tasks. Each small step you take brings you closer to your bigger goal, and celebrating these milestones helps maintain a positive mindset.
- **Stay Flexible**: Sometimes things won't go as planned, and that's okay. A positive mindset means being adaptable and willing to adjust your goals as circumstances change.

g. Mindfulness and Meditation

Mindfulness practices can help you stay grounded, reduce stress, and maintain a positive outlook. By being present in the moment and letting go of worries about the past or future, you can cultivate a greater sense of peace and optimism.

- **Meditation**: Regular meditation helps train the brain to focus on the present and let go of negative thought patterns. Even just 10 minutes of meditation a day can improve mental clarity and emotional resilience.
- **Mindful Breathing**: When you feel stressed or overwhelmed, practice mindful breathing to calm your mind. Take slow, deep breaths and focus on the sensation of the air entering and leaving your body. This simple practice can help shift your mindset from anxiety to calm.

4. Overcoming Obstacles to a Positive Mindset

Despite your best efforts, there will be times when maintaining a positive mindset is difficult. Life's challenges can sometimes feel overwhelming, and it's easy to slip into negative thinking. However, recognizing these obstacles and learning how to overcome them is essential to cultivating a lasting positive mindset.

a. Dealing with Setbacks and Failures

Failure is an inevitable part of life, but it doesn't have to derail your positive mindset. Instead, view setbacks as opportunities for growth and learning.

- **Embrace a Growth Mindset**: When you encounter failure, remind yourself that it's not a reflection of your worth or abilities. Instead, it's a chance to learn, grow, and improve. Ask yourself, "What can I learn from this experience?"
- **Practice Patience**: Change and growth take time. Be patient with yourself as you navigate challenges and setbacks. Remember, progress isn't always linear, but with perseverance, you'll move forward.

b. Coping with Negative Influences

Even with a positive mindset, you may encounter people or situations that bring negativity into your life. It's important to develop strategies for dealing with these influences without letting them undermine your mindset.

- **Set Boundaries**: Protect your mental space by setting boundaries with negative people or environments. If someone consistently brings negativity into your life, consider limiting your interactions with them or addressing the issue directly.
- **Stay Focused on Your Goals**: When faced with negativity, refocus your attention on your personal goals and the progress you're making. This helps to reinforce your positive mindset and keeps you moving in the right direction.

The Impact of positivity on success

Introduction

Positivity is often seen as a soft skill, but its impact on success—both personal and professional—is undeniable. This section explores how a positive mindset can influence decision-making, resilience, leadership, and overall performance. By understanding and applying positivity in daily life, individuals can create a foundation for long-term success.

The Science Behind Positivity

Numerous studies in psychology and neuroscience reveal that a positive mindset does more than just boost morale. It has been linked to:

- **Enhanced problem-solving abilities**: Positivity broadens our cognitive range, making us more creative and better at solving problems.
- **Improved health**: People with a positive outlook tend to have lower stress levels, which contributes to better physical and mental health.
- **Increased resilience**: Positive thinking helps individuals bounce back from challenges more quickly.

This scientific backing emphasizes the practical benefits of maintaining a positive outlook, not just for personal well-being, but also for achieving professional goals.

How Positivity Fuels Success in Business

In the world of business, success is often about how well you can navigate challenges, and positivity plays a pivotal role in this. Here's how:

1. **Better Decision-Making**: A positive mindset allows individuals to approach situations calmly, without being overwhelmed by stress. This leads to better, more calculated decisions that aren't clouded by negativity or fear.
2. **Increased Productivity**: Positive people are more likely to stay motivated and productive. They tend to view challenges as opportunities rather than obstacles, which keeps them moving forward, even when tasks become difficult.
3. **Stronger Relationships**: Success in business often depends on relationships—with clients, employees, and partners. Positivity fosters trust, collaboration, and loyalty, leading to long-lasting, productive business relationships.

4. **Leadership and Influence**: Great leaders are those who inspire and motivate. A positive leader sets the tone for the entire organization, creating an environment where innovation thrives, and employees feel supported and valued.

Cultivating Positivity in Your Daily Routine

To reap the benefits of positivity, it needs to be cultivated intentionally. Here are practical steps to help foster a positive mindset:

- **Gratitude Practice**: Regularly acknowledging the good in your life helps shift your focus from problems to opportunities. Start with a simple habit of writing down three things you're grateful for each day.
- **Mindfulness and Meditation**: Mindfulness practices reduce stress and help maintain a positive outlook by allowing you to stay present and reduce negative rumination.
- **Surround Yourself with Positive Influences**: The people you spend time with impact your mindset. Surrounding yourself with positive, supportive individuals can help you maintain an optimistic attitude.
- **Affirmations and Positive Self-talk**: The way you speak to yourself matters. Positive affirmations and self-talk can reshape your mindset, giving you the confidence to overcome obstacles and keep striving for success.

Overcoming Challenges with a Positive Mindset

Even with the best intentions, challenges are inevitable. However, positivity can help you approach them with resilience and creativity:

- **Reframing Problems**: Instead of viewing problems as roadblocks, try reframing them as learning opportunities. This shift in perspective can help you approach challenges with a solution-oriented mindset.
- **Developing Resilience**: Positivity doesn't mean ignoring difficulties; it means facing them with a belief that they can be overcome. Resilient individuals are those who use setbacks as a springboard for future success.

Case Studies: Successful Leaders Who Embraced Positivity

Many successful business leaders attribute their achievements to maintaining a positive outlook:

- **Richard Branson**: Known for his enthusiasm and optimism, Branson has built an empire by fostering a positive company culture and embracing challenges with a can-do attitude.
- **Oprah Winfrey**: Oprah's journey from hardship to becoming a media mogul is a testament to the power of positive thinking. Her belief in herself and her vision allowed her to rise above obstacles and inspire millions.

These examples demonstrate how positivity can be a driving force behind sustained success.

Techniques for Fostering a Positive Outlook

Reframing Negative Thoughts

A positive outlook is not simply about ignoring challenges or pretending everything is perfect. It's about how we choose to interpret and respond to the situations we face. One of the most effective techniques for fostering a positive mindset is learning how to reframe negative thoughts. This method involves shifting your perspective and finding ways to view negative situations in a more constructive light. Below is an in-depth exploration of how reframing works, why it's effective, and practical steps for applying this technique.

---

1. Understanding Negative Thought Patterns

We all experience negative thoughts, whether they stem from personal setbacks, challenges, or failures. However, when negative thoughts become habitual, they can lead to a cycle of self-doubt, stress, and anxiety, which hinder productivity and emotional well-being. Common negative thought patterns include:

- **All-or-Nothing Thinking**: Seeing things in black and white terms, such as "If I fail, I'm a complete failure."
- **Overgeneralization**: Assuming that because one bad thing happened, it will keep happening.
- **Catastrophizing**: Expecting the worst possible outcome from every situation.

Recognizing these thought patterns is the first step toward overcoming them.

2. The Power of Reframing

Reframing involves taking a step back and consciously shifting your interpretation of a situation. The goal isn't to ignore reality but to adjust your perspective to focus on opportunities for growth, lessons, or alternative outcomes.

For example:

- Instead of thinking, "I failed at this task," reframe it as, "I learned what doesn't work and can use that knowledge to improve next time."
- Rather than saying, "I'm terrible at this," you could say, "I'm still learning, and with more practice, I'll get better."

Reframing encourages you to replace negative assumptions with more balanced, productive ones.

3. Practical Steps to Reframing Negative Thoughts

Step 1: Identify the Negative Thought The first step in reframing is self-awareness. Pay attention to the automatic negative thoughts that arise throughout your day. These might come in the form of internal dialogues, assumptions, or worst-case scenario thinking.

Step 2: Challenge the Thought Once you've identified a negative thought, ask yourself:

- Is this thought rational or an emotional reaction?
- What evidence do I have to support or refute this thought?
- Could there be another explanation or perspective that I haven't considered?

By questioning the validity of negative thoughts, you can start to break them down.

Step 3: Create a Balanced Reframe Now that you've identified and challenged your negative thought, the next step is to create a reframe that is realistic and positive. This doesn't mean making overly optimistic statements but finding a perspective that acknowledges the challenge while also highlighting potential benefits or solutions.

Step 4: Practice Regularly Reframing is a skill that requires practice. The more consistently you challenge and reframe your negative thoughts, the easier it becomes to foster a positive mindset. Over time, this shift in thinking will become automatic, leading to greater resilience and emotional balance.

4. Using Gratitude to Reinforce Reframing

Practicing gratitude can be a powerful reinforcement for reframing negative thoughts. When you focus on what you're grateful for, it becomes easier to find the positive aspects of difficult situations. Regularly reflecting on things you're thankful for can help shift your mindset from what's going wrong to what's going well.

- **Daily Gratitude Journals**: Write down three things you're grateful for every day. These can be as simple as a nice conversation or as significant as a major accomplishment.
- **Gratitude in Challenging Moments**: When you face a setback, try to find something you can appreciate about the situation, even if it's just the opportunity to learn or grow.

5. The Impact of Language on Reframing

The words we use, even in our internal dialogue, shape our perception of reality. The language of negativity ("I can't," "This is impossible," "I'm terrible at this") reinforces a fixed mindset, making it harder to adopt a positive outlook. Instead, replace limiting language with empowering alternatives:

- **From** "I'm not good at this" **to** "I'm still learning, and I will get better with time."

- **From** "This is too hard" **to** "This is a challenge, but I've faced challenges before and succeeded."

By changing your language, you signal to your brain that you are capable of growth and improvement.

6. Visualizing Positive Outcomes

Visualization is another tool that complements reframing. When faced with negative thoughts about the future, use visualization to imagine positive outcomes. By mentally rehearsing success, you're not only preparing yourself for the possibility of things going right, but you're also reinforcing your belief in positive outcomes.

How to Practice Visualization:

- Find a quiet space, close your eyes, and take a few deep breaths.
- Visualize yourself handling a challenging situation with confidence and ease.
- Picture the steps you'll take to achieve a positive outcome, and imagine the emotions you'll feel once you succeed.

Visualization helps your brain create a mental roadmap for success, making it easier to stay positive when challenges arise.

7. Surrounding Yourself with Positivity

The environment and people you surround yourself with play a crucial role in maintaining a positive outlook. Spending time with people who uplift and inspire you can help counterbalance the negativity you may face in other areas of life. Similarly, curating an environment that promotes optimism can make it easier to stay positive.

- **Positive Social Circles**: Build relationships with individuals who encourage you, celebrate your successes, and offer constructive feedback.
- **Uplifting Media**: Limit exposure to negative media and instead focus on content that inspires, educates, and motivates you.

Conclusion

In the journey of writing this book, we've explored the many dimensions of thinking like a businessman. Whether you're aspiring to start your own business, excel in your career, or simply adopt a more strategic approach to life, the core principles remain the same: clarity of vision, resilience in the face of setbacks, a relentless focus on problem-solving, and the ability to adapt and innovate.

Thinking like a businessman isn't just about mastering financial statements or developing the perfect business plan. It's a mindset that requires an entrepreneurial spirit, the ability to see opportunities where others see challenges, and the discipline to stay focused on long-term goals. It involves calculated risks, thoughtful decision-making, and a constant desire for growth, both personally and professionally.

As you move forward, remember that every successful businessman didn't achieve greatness overnight. Behind every achievement are stories of hard work, failures, and lessons learned. The key is to embrace those lessons, remain adaptable, and continue refining your mindset. Being a businessman is about persistence—turning every obstacle into an opportunity for improvement and growth.

I encourage you to take the tools, strategies, and insights shared in this book and apply them to your unique situation. Stay curious, keep learning, and never shy away from challenges. Most importantly, think like a businessman not only in your professional life but in how you approach all aspects of life—with vision, purpose, and determination.

Your journey is just beginning. Now, armed with the mindset of a businessman, go out and make it happen. Success awaits those who are willing to think big, work hard, and never stop striving for better.

Good luck, and remember—you are the architect of your own success.

Encouragement to adopt the business mindset.

In summary, adopting a business mindset empowers you to take ownership of your life, see opportunities in challenges, think long-term, and continuously grow. It equips you with the resilience to overcome obstacles, the strategic thinking to achieve your goals, and the networking skills to build meaningful relationships.

The mindset of a businessman isn't confined to the corporate world. It's a way of thinking and acting that can help you achieve success in all areas of your life. Whether you're building a business, advancing your career, or simply aiming for personal fulfillment, the principles of this mindset will guide you toward lasting success.

Now is the time to embrace this way of thinking and take control of your future. By committing to the business mindset, you're committing to a life of growth, achievement, and purpose.

www.ingramcontent.com/pod-product-compliance
Lightning Source LLC
Chambersburg PA
CBHW050258230526
45471CB00005B/1931